DANCING
AND
CLEVER COYOTES

DANCING OTTERS
AND
CLEVER COYOTES

Using Animal Energies
the Native American Way

Gary Buffalo Horn Man
and
Sherry Firedancer

Skyhorse Publishing

Skyhorse Publishing books may be purchased in bulk at special discounts for sales promotion, corporate gifts, fund-raising, or educational purposes. Special editions can also be created to specifications. For details, contact the Special Sales Department, Skyhorse Publishing, 555 Eighth Avenue, Suite 903, New York, NY 10018 or info@skyhorsepublishing.com.

www.skyhorsepublishing.com

10 9 8 7 6 5 4 3 2 1

Library of Congress Cataloging-in-Publication Data

Buffalo Horn Man, Gary.
Dancing otters and clever coyotes : using animal energies, the Native American way / Gary Buffalo Horn Man and Sherry Firedancer.
p. cm.
ISBN 978-1-60239-637-1 (pbk. : alk. paper)
1. Indians of North America--Rites and ceremonies. 2. Indian philosophy--North America. 3. Animals--Symbolic aspects--North America. 4. Human-animal relationships--North America. 5. Animals--North America--Miscellanea. 6. New Age movement--North America. I. Firedancer, Sherry. II. Title.
E98.R53B84 2009
299.7--dc22

2009017869

Printed in China

• •

This work is dedicated to all those beings whose lives have been taken by humans, and through human activity, without respect or sacred intent. In these pages and in our hearts, you are remembered with love and honor.

Also, we wish to thank our medicine teacher for pointing his finger at us.

—Gary and Sherry

• •

Table of Contents

INTRODUCTION

Greetings to Old Friends and New Readers! We are so very excited about this wonderful new edition, *Dancing Otters and Clever Coyotes*, with all of its beautiful pictures and bright colors. Our old friends will know an earlier version of this book by the title *Animal Energies*. We trust you will be pleased with this revised and expanded edition of your old dog-eared companion. We hope that new readers will find this book interesting, informative, and useful in your lives, so that it will become a trusted guide to a new way of thinking about, and connecting with, all the other beings with whom we share the planet. And of course, we hope everyone will find pleasure in simply reading its pages for the information and stories they contain.

How This Book Came to Be

The authors of your book are Gary Buffalo Horn Man and Sherry Firedancer. We are devoted partners in life and work, living a quiet life on a rural mountainside in West Virginia, with no visible neighbors other than the wildlife who share our forest land. We operate a mail-order catalog business from home and regularly include ceremony in the course of doing our work and living our lives.

We named our business Dancing Otter in honor of Sherry's medicine name and Gary's great affinity for Otters and his love of play, and because the work we do is so much fun. We sell Native American artwork, craft supplies, and ceremonial herbs, specializing in the sale of animal fetishes hand-carved by the Zuni Indians of New Mexico. We truly enjoy providing a unique service to people through our written words and our high-quality, low-priced products. We feel good about the things we sell and are grateful that proceeds from Dancing Otter over the last seventeen years have enabled us to acquire a little house and a small parcel of land. Our home has become a habitat and sanctuary for a large variety of birds, mammals, reptiles, and insects who visit our backyard for regular offerings of seed, suet, corn, and other tasty edibles.

In the course of doing business and selling our wares at powwows and other events, we were constantly asked for more information about what the animals represent, and about how people could work with the energies of particular animals to promote learning and healing in their lives. When we displayed summary cards with our merchandise, we got even more questions from a logjam of knowledge-seekers copying down what was written on the cards. It seemed obvious that there were a lot of people searching for this kind of lore.

In 1992, we self-published *Animal Energies* as a way of sharing knowledge that has been given to us through our direct encounters with animals, Native American stories we've heard, ceremonies and teachings we've been given by the elders we have been privileged to work with, and intuition we have acquired by spending time on the land, watching and listening. In the course of our travels, we have had opportunities to talk with many people, and to learn of their experiences and the lessons they have received from our planetary cohabitants.

Since publishing our first book, we have received hundreds of letters, e-mails, and phone calls from readers sharing their own stories and insight. One caller a few months ago was Sally van Haitsma, an agent with Castiglia Literary Agency in Del Mar, California. Sally had discovered *Animal Energies* at a friend's house, liked what she read, and wondered if we might want her to look for an outside publisher for our work. At that time, we had sold over 100,000 copies of our book—a number that makes us feel truly honored and humble—but most of those sales had come about through word-of-mouth advertising and a couple of book distributors. We are hoping that, with editing and promotional help from Skyhorse Publishing in New York, our even-better book will now find its way into the hands of many more readers. In preparing *Dancing Otters and Clever Coyotes*, we have done more research, read more stories, talked with more people, pondered and discussed the messages that each animal shares with us and, of course, asked Spirit for help with this project.

What This Book Contains

The Animals

At the beginning of this book are descriptions of 58 wild animals inhabiting the North American continent, along with fabulous photographs. We present data about the habits and habitats of each mammal, bird, reptile, and insect, and share anecdotal material wherever we can. We then describe how each being's unique gifts can teach us something that we

3

need to know. Finally, we explore how the vulnerabilities or blind spots of each can communicate warnings to us of dangers or shortcomings.

If some of our interpretations seem right for you, that is good. If few seem to fit with your view of the world, that too is good, for we all are different. Our intention is to offer you ways of thinking about your encounters with animals—physically and spiritually—that you may not have considered before. Understanding animal medicine can help us all to be more aware of our own strengths and weaknesses and to see how we fit into the Circle of Creation. Reflections from the world around us provide valuable clues for understanding what is inside ourselves, showing us how to change our beliefs so we can attain the peace and love that we all seek.

Encounters with Animals

Following the alphabetical presentation of animal energies are two stories describing our personal encounters with animals, which we hope will illustrate how people can learn important lessons about themselves by virtue of such interactions. One is Gary's amusing account of his close encounter with a "reindeer," and the other describes Sherry's interaction with a bird family nesting on our front porch.

Our notion of an "animal encounter" is crossing paths with an animal in some way that really catches your attention and causes you to think about how that meeting relates to certain aspects of your life. The encounter could be in the physical world or in a dream or meditation, or an animal could appear as a sign or a guide in some other way. As an example, Sherry "once spent an afternoon out on the land, sitting in the middle of a grove of young trees, just being, and watching Spiders. Observing their web-weaving compelled me to consider at length how the tapestry of my own life had become torn and how I might be able to mend it. It was an important day in my past."

Whatever the nature of your encounter with an animal, if you feel in your heart that there is a lesson to be learned, take the time to contemplate it. Where were you? What was going on in your life? What were you thinking at the time of the encounter? What thoughts did you have following the event? Perhaps the messages suggested in our book will help you interpret your encounter in a way that is meaningful to you. Ultimately, it is your personal relationship with the animal—your unique history with it and your innate beliefs about it—that determines exactly what energies it has to share with you.

If there is an animal with whom you have always felt an affinity, you might do well to determine what it has been trying to tell you for so long. If there is a matter on which you need guidance, you may find it beneficial to seek out a particular animal whose medicine knowledge could shed light on the situation. If your encounter happens to be with an animal not included in this book, we encourage you to research its ways and read stories about it since an animal's message is often revealed in how it interacts with the world.

Original Stories Told in the Native American Style

Following our personal accounts, you will find two original stories that Gary wrote. Both take place in earlier times, when animals and people could communicate directly with

5

one another, and both describe the poignant circumstances that caused that to change. They are told in the Native way of storytelling, which often teaches by means of allegory.

Because survival required that they live in close-knit groups, Native people were careful not to violate tribal standards, for to do so was to risk ridicule or ostracism. With no written codes of law to guide them, parents taught cultural mores to their young ones through stories that demonstrated what was and was not acceptable. By using a familiar animal to illustrate a point, a story could bring its lesson to mind every time the listener saw that animal. Most tribes had designated storytellers, individuals assigned to keep the tribe's history and teachings within their heads and hearts. These people were accorded great honor within the tribe and throughout the broader community with whom they shared their tales.

The Smudging Ceremony

Also included in this book is a description of a smudging ceremony we were taught by an Ojibway elder. The ceremony uses the smoke from burning herbs to cleanse one's mind, body, emotions, and spirit, thus opening one's whole being to new energies and ideas. This way of praying might aid you in deciphering what you can learn from an animal encounter.

Why This Book Is Important

All things put here by Creator have a place and a purpose and, as such, deserve respect and honor. The Sun and the Earth combine energy and form to make life possible. Spirit infuses all things to make life meaningful and magical. The Sacred Circle of Life is the balance and the dance of all the seen and unseen. It is the natural harmony of all the different beings living their lives in a sacred way: stones, plants, trees, animals, insects, people, bacteria, the land, the water, the stars, the Earth . . .

Understanding and respect are the natural outcomes of following the rhythms of the Earth and celebrating them with ceremony. Disrespect arises when the Sacred Circle that binds all things together breaks.

If a person's circle is broken in one place, he may respect all of the animate beings sharing the Earth but he can crush and mine rock with no consciousness, move and shape the stones without care.

If one's circle is broken in another place, respect for plant relatives is lost. Old-growth forests become timber. Rainforests become grazing land for cattle. Plants become weeds, useless pests to be destroyed.

If someone's circle is broken in still another place, she loses respect for our insect relatives. She would never disregard a plant or harm an animal, but bugs? Spray and splat!

If their circles are broken somewhere else, people consider the lives and needs of our animal brothers and sisters to be meaningless, and they can see them only for how they can be of "use"—for fur, food, money, or sport.

If one's circle is broken in yet another place, the lives of various people become worthless: the poor, the rich, the black, the white, the red, the yellow, the foreigner, the immigrant, the stranger, the enemy, the old, the young, the sick, family, non-family, men, women . . .

7

And if one's circle is broken in the most fundamental place, then respect for oneself is gone.

For too many people, circles are broken in several places or shattered completely. But if we can repair the Sacred Hoop, we can strengthen our families, our communities, our environments, and ourselves. We can find our place in the Web of Creation, and restore the knowledge that Native peoples living close to the Earth have had for thousands of years: that every individual person, as well as every stone, plant, and animal, has a place in the Sacred Circle of Creation. All contribute to the whole through gifts and talents uniquely their own. In essence, all beings in this world are Great Mystery wearing different faces.

This basic but profound interconnectedness enables the silent teachings of the animals to reach our minds and allows their messages to touch our hearts. We hope that, in some way, our work can enhance human ability to accept the guidance of our animal kin and to comprehend their truths, thereby enriching all our lives. Let us be open to the wisdom that comes from understanding and to the happiness that celebration of all life brings.

We wish a good life and great happiness to all in the Sacred Circle.

Aho, Brothers and Sisters, it is good!

—Sherry Firedancer and Gary Buffalo Horn Man
March 2009

Dancing Otters
and
Clever Coyotes

THE ANIMALS

We are all related

All heat comes from Father Sun. All form and substance come from Mother Earth. Without the Sun, the Earth would be a cold, lifeless place. Without the Earth, the Sun would burn but touch nothing. Great Mystery Which Moves In All Things created the Sun and the Earth and they became lovers. The formless fire penetrated and caressed the cold firmament, and the Mother became pregnant. She gave birth to water, and to stone, and to air. Great Mystery moved through her children, and then they too made love. The ocean stroked and caressed the stone and gave rise to a new being. This being, warmed by the Sun's fire, nurtured by the Mother's water, and composed of the Mother's body, was the first life.

Great Spirit, in a never-ending dance of love, made this life fertile, and brought forth all the many beings that have been, are, and will be. All life is of the Mother's water and her stone body, heated by the sacred fire of Father Sun. All that we humans think we own is a gift of love to us, the love of Creator. It is called evolution, and it is called creation; both are right. For what is DNA but the atoms, the smallest pieces, of the many different kinds of rocks and air? It is carbon, nitrogen, oxygen, sulfur, hydrogen, sodium, and on and on—stones and air, floating in water.

We get all of our energy from what we eat—plants and animals that eat plants, beings fed by Father Sun. We burn this food for our human fire, 98.6 degrees Fahrenheit, the same fire that burns in Father Sun. This is *what* we are. *Who* we are is a mystery, a Great Mystery. All we know is this: We are born of love, composed of gifts of love, and put here to honor that love and its source.

The animals, fish, and insects of this world are our brothers and sisters. They are made of the same substance as we, burning with the same fire. The Spirit Which Moves In All Things gives all beings in the Circle of Life different shapes, qualities, gifts, and powers. If we can reach a level of consciousness where we are aware of these truths, we can freely communicate with all parts of Creation, as well as with the Creator. We will reclaim the knowledge that has been forgotten: that we are all related, and all One.

Alligator

ALLIGATOR'S MESSAGE:
Take care of survival and emergency needs.

ALLIGATOR'S WARNING:
You may need to change your circumstances.

Behavior and Habitat

Alligator has walked on the Earth Mother for millions of years. These reptiles hide themselves in water and mud, waiting for an unsuspecting creature to happen by, and then—*snap*!—the powerful jaws close and all hope is lost. They will eat any animal they can swallow whole and, if they can't swallow it, they will tear it into bite-size pieces with their eighty teeth. The largest Alligator on record was more than 19 feet long. It could easily have pulled a cow or a horse into the water and killed it. The muscles that close their jaws are extremely powerful, while the muscles that open them are very weak, allowing an Alligator's mouth to be held closed by a human hand. Alligator's seeming sluggishness is transformed into startling speed when a hungry one goes after prey. It is also a surprisingly quick swimmer, propelling itself through the water with the help of its powerfully muscular body and tail.

When we toured the Louisiana Bayou a few years ago, our guide encouraged us to hold his young pet Alligator, Julie, who had become accustomed to the attentions of human visitors and enjoyed having her head stroked. She was only about three feet long and no more than fifteen inches in circumference, but she was solid muscle through and through. She exuded raw power; we were both quite sure that if she had wanted to get down, there would have been no stopping her.

Alligators come together only for reproduction. For a reptile, the female's maternal nature is extraordinary. She lays 20 to 60 eggs in a nesting mound, covers it with vegetation, and then stays to guard the eggs during the ten-week incubation period. The young are born as fully formed Alligators, who begin eating anything they can, starting with insects, frogs, and crustaceans and work up to fish, turtles, and mammals. Mother and offspring stay together for a year or longer. Alligators dig deep burrows when the water is high so they can have a wet alcove to retreat to during dry seasons. The reservoirs thus created also provide water for other animals.

How Alligator's Medicine Gifts Help Us

The power of Alligator is its ability to survive. Except for humans, who hunted them almost to extinction to make shoes and purses, Alligators have no enemies. They can eat almost anything and have existed in their present form for a very long time. They thrive in heat and will hibernate if the weather gets cold. If Alligator has come to you, either in the physical world or in a dream or vision, it may be trying to tell you to take care of yourself to ensure your basic survival. Are you eating food that nourishes you so you might live a long and healthy life? On a practical level, are you prepared in your home and your car so you can survive an emergency? On a spiritual level, do you live somewhere that is conducive to your inner needs as well as your physical well-being? Is your home a haven during the "dry" seasons in your life?

How Alligator Can Warn Us of Danger

Alligators will generally avoid people, but one that becomes out of balance with its own nature could very well stray too close to human habitation, especially as we encroach on their space. If an Alligator were to get hungry enough to eat garbage or—alas—pets, it would undoubtedly be destroyed. So if the unfriendly Alligator from your nightmare is now in your backyard, ask yourself why. Are you out of balance with your own nature? Are you perhaps moving in circles or working at a job that is contrary to what you believe in? Is your very survival on some level in jeopardy? The message from Alligator may be to move to a place of safety before you lose your struggle to survive.

Ant

ANT'S MESSAGE:
You need to find your role in life.

ANT'S WARNING:
Don't be a mindless automaton.

Behavior and Habitat

Ants are amazing creatures. They do many of the things that we do. They have agriculture; some species grow fungus underground. They tend livestock; some Ants farm aphids, from which they get sugary nectar. They go to war. They migrate. They have complex societies, with many different jobs performed by individuals with specialized skills. They construct vast networks of tunnels and other structures in which to live. And all of this is accomplished with a nervous system that is small and simple, lacking the complexity of human anatomy.

As an example of their coordinated interaction, consider the Weaver Ant. They live primarily in trees, but instead of digging burrows in the bark as most insects do, these Ants build housing chambers out of leaves they glue together. Because the leaves are heavy compared to the insects, the Weaver Ants form multiple living chains between leaves they have selected,

and, with some Ants holding other Ants, they cooperate in pulling the leaves together until they are positioned just right. The silk that serves as glue is a substance produced only by their larvae, so other Ants bring larvae from existing chambers to the building site and then use them as living tools to apply the glue. The larvae are then returned unharmed to their chambers, while the builders finish bending and molding the leaves into the structures in which they all live.

How Ant's Medicine Gifts Help Us

The power of Ant medicine is teamwork. Ant society has an organization that is unparalleled in the animal world. In different species of Ants there are warriors, breeders, farmers, livestock herders, parents, workers, builders, slave drivers, raiders, and others. Some Ants will fight, some will dig tunnels, some will carry leaves for miles—all working for the

good of the community. Each Ant knows the role it must play in order to ensure the health and survival of the entire colony, and it will perform its duties with total loyalty to the whole.

If Ant has marched into your awareness, a message it might have for you is to look around at how you are being asked to fit into the big picture. Creator may want you to play a specific role for the well-being of your family, your community, or the Earth Mother. Follow Ant to determine what job you can best perform and do your work as well as you possibly can, always keeping in mind that you are contributing to something greater than yourself.

How Ant Can Warn Us of Danger

Ant's message could be a warning that you are conforming a bit too much to what others expect of you. Are you following the group mindlessly and ignoring a promising new direction? Even society-bound Ant knows when the time is right to break away from the colony and start a new hill.

Antelope

ANTELOPE'S MESSAGE:

You may need to move with speed and clear vision.

ANTELOPE'S WARNING:

Pay attention to what is directly in front of you.

Behavior and Habitat

Before the Europeans arrived, there were an estimated 30 to 40 million Pronghorn Antelope in North America. As with the buffalo, they were overhunted, until as few as 30,000 remained. Conservation efforts have raised their numbers to nearly one million today. Antelope live in the grasslands and brushlands of western states between Canada and Mexico. They graze on grasses until the snows come, and then they subsist on sagebrush. Antelope generally weigh between 90 and 150 pounds and their average life span in the wild is about ten years. They have horns, not antlers, and are the only animals in the world who annually shed their horns. The white hairs on Antelope's rump grow in unique rosette designs that identify the animals to one another and also help herds traveling at night to keep together. These ruminant

animals have very keen eyesight and unusually sharp hearing, enabling them to detect movement from miles away.

Pronghorn Antelope are the fastest land animals in North America, able to attain speeds of over 50 miles per hour. They can also sustain a fast run, though not at top speed, for long distances. They like to race each other and to run along with any fast-moving object. When a newborn is four days old, it can outrun an adult horse, and by the time it is four weeks old, it can keep pace with its herd. As fast as they are, Antelope cannot jump very well, and the fences erected all across the western states for cattle pose barriers to the movement of their herds. Being unable or at least reluctant to jump, they try instead to crawl underneath them.

How Antelope's Medicine Gifts Help Us

Antelope shares with us the gifts of clear vision and quick motion. They can see things coming across a very long distance and can act with fantastic alacrity to get out of harm's way. If Antelope has sprinted into your territory, it may be saying that you should be prepared to move with utmost speed to get where you need to go before something goes awry. Antelope don't wait for a threat to approach; as soon as they sense danger, they take action. You might seek the gifts of Antelope if you see clearly what you must do to move forward but need some help to do it faster.

How Antelope Can Warn Us of Danger

Antelope won't help you run from something that you cannot perceive. Although an Antelope can see a moving predator for miles, it might very easily stumble upon one a few feet away that is hidden and still. Antelope may have a warning for you that while your gaze is off in the distance, it is the thing right next to you that needs your attention.

Armadillo

ARMADILLO'S MESSAGE:

You're protected if you stay balanced and aware.

ARMADILLO'S WARNING:

Don't be careless in your endeavors.

Behavior and Habitat

Armadillo means "little armored one" in Spanish. These curious creatures live where the weather is warm in our southern states. They can measure 32 inches in length and weigh up to 18 pounds. Strong legs and huge front claws are used for digging, and long, sticky tongues extract ants and termites from their underground tunnels. Armadillos have many different burrows, which they share with members of the same sex. They hunt at night, primarily for insects, but they will also eat small animals, birds' eggs, fruit, roots, and carrion. They have an acute sense of smell but poor sight and hearing.

Nine-banded Armadillo females always give birth to four genetically identical young that have developed from the same egg. Baby Armadillos have soft shells, like human fingernails, which harden as the animal grows hard bony plates, arranged in bands, under flexible lizard-like skin. This process creates the solid, protective shell that gives Armadillo its unique appearance. Contrary to popular belief, most Armadillos cannot curl up into an armored ball. Only one of the 20 or so subspecies, the Three-banded Armadillo, is able to do that, since the other types are covered with too many hard plates to allow them to curl. Instead, these Armadillos hope their armored shells will defend them while they scuttle away through thick, thorny brush or dig themselves a hole in which to hide. Some Armadillos, when threatened, will lie flat on the ground, and tuck their legs under their shields, or they might try to startle a predator by jumping straight up very quickly.

How Armadillo's Medicine Gifts Help Us

Armadillo's medicine derives from its ability to live life and conduct business in a protected and safe way. An Armadillo cannot easily be harmed as long as it remains aware and remembers its natural ways. Are your physical and psychic spaces appropriately shielded from circumstances that could lead to your undoing? If Armadillo is meandering in your direction, its message may be that you need to protect yourself from people or events that could throw you off balance and make you vulnerable.

How Armadillo Can Warn Us of Danger

An Armadillo who becomes out of balance with its own natural way of being can stray too far from its dens or sleep on its back, leaving its unprotected underside exposed to predators. Armadillo shows us that when we are in balance and following the path that Creator is laying out for us, we are safe and secure, but when we leave that sacred walk, we could encounter hardship through our own carelessness or lack of awareness.

Badger

> ## BADGER'S MESSAGE:
> Organize and take charge in order to free your energies.
>
> ## BADGER'S WARNING:
> You may be stuck in a negative pattern.

Behavior and Habitat

Badgers are short, stocky members of the weasel family, two to three feet long but only about one foot high. Their diet includes a wide variety of roots, plants, nuts, and berries, as well as many insects and small animals. Powerful legs and long front claws enable them to dig five or six feet down with remarkable speed when they need to get underground; burrowing prey are no match for them. Their senses of smell and hearing are excellent but their sight is poor, so family members mark each other with scent for recognition. As Badgers are largely nocturnal, the unique patterns of light and dark fur striping their faces also aid recognition in the dark. They tend to be rather inactive during cold winter months.

Badgers have erroneously been considered aggressive be-cause they will fight fiercely in self-defense. They have few serious enemies, however, except for humans. Coyotes have even been known to follow a Badger digging for rodents since Badgers are not adept at running down prey that escapes, so the coyote just might pick up an easy meal.

Badgers live in simple but extremely clean, well-kept dens. They change their bedding often, backing carefully into their dens with straw so as not to make a mess in the process. They pay close attention to details within their home environments. In a volume of short stories entitled *Between Man and Beast*, compiled by Gilbert and John Phelps, there is an amusing account of a proper British pet Badger named Nikki. According to author Molly Burkett, Nikki kept the family's house perfectly tidy by routinely clearing all flat surfaces of anything placed on them—including the dining-room table, if they weren't careful. Evidently, Nikki was particularly offended by Molly's mother's placement of new plants in the flower garden, for she dug up every one and lined them all up in three neat rows under Mum's bed.

How Badger's Medicine Gifts Help Us

Badger brings us the gifts of tidiness and organization. They are fastidious about their surroundings and will correct any disorder quickly. If Badger has come to you in some way, it may be saying that you need to concentrate on maintaining an orderly environment to better facilitate your day-to-day living. Many people live by the adage that it is efficient to have a special place for everything and for that item to be in its designated place when it is needed. Badger can teach about efficiency in many ways, because once you have taken charge of your space, you can better manage your time. And if you clear your mind of clutter as well, you will have the personal wherewithal to devote more effort to all aspects of your busy life—family, friends, job, ceremonies and the spiritual realm, and everything else that fills your days.

How Badger Can Warn Us of Danger

A Badger will fight to the death if it is cornered. While this may be a commendable trait in the wild, men exploited this quality in the so-called sport of Badger-baiting. Captured Badgers were put into small enclosed areas with a dog or dogs, and bets were placed on the outcomes of the fights. Have you become trapped in a pattern that once served you well but is now damaging? Is there a characteristic you defend fiercely even though it may be harming a relationship? If you have been backed into a corner because of a blind spot, Badger could be warning you that a change of behavior is in order if you don't want to be used or abused.

Bat

BAT'S MESSAGE:
Look around you for opportunities to be of service.

BAT'S WARNING:
Pause to refocus on your goals.

Behavior and Habitat

There are many different species of Bats widespread throughout warm and temperate climates in both Americas; in cooler regions, they hibernate through cold seasons. There are Bats who eat insects or drink blood; others are vegetarian, with a diet of nectar or fruit. Generally, female Bats bear only one offspring a year. Their multitudes are maintained by their longevity, since they can live for 20 years in the wild.

Contrary to popular assumption, Bats see quite well, but because they most often hunt in the dark, they must rely on nonvisual means to find food and move around safely. Their sense of smell is good, but they depend primarily on echolocation, whereby sound waves from the high-pitched chattering

for which they are known bounce back from objects in their flight path. Bats are the only mammals that truly fly. One could call them furry birds, except that their method of flying more closely resembles a swimmer's breast stroke than the flapping of wings. Their unique construction enables them to perform unparalleled acrobatic maneuvers, all in their frenetic search for food.

Studies on Bats found that when they are placed in a refrigerator, they go into an instant state of hibernation and come out unharmed when they are warmed, whether it is a few days or a few months later. (Who thinks up these experiments?) This is unique and amazing for a warm-blooded animal.

We have a Bat house attached high up on the side of a shed. One summer evening, we counted forty Bats leaving the small structure within several minutes, and we might have missed a couple. It was mesmerizing to watch the Bats drop out of the frame, sometimes two or three at a time, fall a few feet, and then set off due south, all following the same pattern like a little flying Bat parade. There is a bit of a guano issue, but we see very few mosquitoes where we live, and that works for us!

How Bat's Medicine Gifts Help Us

All night long, Bats work tirelessly controlling insect populations, which benefits all creatures on the planet, including the nations of those they eat. Mother Bats even go off to their duties with their babies attached to their backs by means of milk teeth. Bat brings to us the ethic of hard work that serves a higher purpose. If Bat is flying around you, it may be suggesting that you need to examine your surroundings to see if there is more work you can do to keep your environment free of those things that could cause harm to yourself, to others, or to Mother Earth.

How Bat Can Warn Us of Danger

If a Bat becomes out of balance with its world, its brain can get scrambled and confused and it will fly into things. Are you crashing into barriers as you try to get what you think you want and need? If so, Bat may be advising you to take a moment to get your bearings, reevaluate the importance of what you are seeking, and then work as hard as you can to create the reality that will best serve your higher self.

Bear

> **BEAR'S MESSAGE:**
> Gifts of strength and wisdom are available to you.
>
> **BEAR'S WARNING:**
> Be aware of limits and warnings.

Behavior and Habitat

There are three species of Bears in North America: Black, Brown, and Polar Bears. The Grizzly and Kodiak are types of Brown Bear. They all eat a wide variety of plants and animals. When food is scarce, all Bears hibernate to at least some extent, with the exception of Polar Bears, who remain active all year and take to snow dens only to give birth and shelter their young. Bears reach sexual maturity at three to five years of age and can live up to 30 years.

Black Bears, despite their name, can be chocolate brown, cinnamon brown, or blue-black. They grow to five feet long and weigh up to 500 pounds, and are by far the most numerous and widespread of the Bear species. Female Black Bears generally give birth to two or three cubs during winter hibernation; the mother wakes up to give birth, bites off the umbilical cords, and promptly goes back into her deep sleep. The cubs, weighing only around ten ounces at birth, do not hibernate, but begin a routine of drinking milk and sleeping normally until their mother awakens and introduces them to the outside world.

Grizzly Bears are usually considered the most fierce and aggressive of all Bears, especially when surprised, cornered, injured, or with cubs. Adult males average six feet in height and can weigh up to 650 pounds. There are an estimated 30,000 Grizzlies in Alaska and Canada, but only about 1,000 living in the lower 48 states. The Kodiak Bear, which can grow to be ten feet long and can weigh 1,500 pounds, is huge even compared to its cousin the Grizzly. The Kodiak Bear takes its name from its home on Kodiak Island off the southwest coast of Alaska.

Members of the Polar Bear family can grow the largest, weighing as much as 1,700 pounds and reaching a standing height of 11 feet. Their paws average 12 inches in length by 10 inches wide. A Polar Bear can knock a 500-pound seal out of the water with one blow. Polar Bears' white-fur camouflage is perfect for hunting on the Arctic ice, but their big black noses are more visible. Thus, when they are stalking seals and waiting for them to come up for air, Polar Bears will sometimes cover their noses with a paw to avoid detection. Excellent swimmers, they have been known to swim as far as 50 miles through icy waters.

Bear's Connection to Native American Culture

Although the specifics of different tribal traditions vary greatly with regard to Bear (entire books have been written

on the subject), one thing remains fairly consistent: Bear has long been an important figure in virtually every Native culture and has played a prominent role in many Native ceremonies. In general, Bear has been considered to be a close relative of humans, since it can stand and walk on two legs, eats many of the same foods that we do, and has very strong maternal instincts.

Many nations of Native people saw Bear as a powerful medicine teacher and considered it highly desirable to have Bear as an ally and spirit helper. Some tribes prayed for medicine dreams that would show Bear to be their guide, and others, such as the Cree, sought dreams about Bear as a way of locating them and receiving permission to hunt them in a sacred way. The Lakota believed that dreams of Bear would give people knowledge of herbs and help make them healers. The Blackfeet viewed Bear as a powerful ally and often carved knife handles from the animal's jaw bones. And Brother Bear has always been the most prevalent and popular of all Zuni fetishes, as people seek a way to work with Bear's energy without the risk of being eaten.

The Assiniboine, among other tribes, had a Bear society to which only persons who dreamed of the Bear could gain admittance. The society would never eat Bear flesh, and in battle its warriors dressed and painted themselves to resemble Bear. Other Bear societies, such as those of the Crow nation, would eat Bear meat as a way of accessing its power.

Other tribes, however, were wary of Bear's power. The Navajo felt that Bear was too powerful and fearsome a being to have contact with, except under extreme circumstances. They would hunt Bear only if it meant not starving, believing that too much contact with Bear could make one crazy. The Shoshone thought that Bear was too quick to anger and would make a poor medicine ally for family men. The Inuit believed that Bear medicine was good for boys, but not for girls because it would make them unforgiving.

How Bear's Medicine Gifts Help Us

As Bear is our closest relative among all the animals in North America, its medicine gift is to be a teacher to us two-leggeds. Woven throughout Native American lore are examples of interactions in which Bear shows people how to walk their paths with strength and understanding, and without fear. Bear can serve as a mirror reflecting to us how we might walk upright in a balanced way on the Earth Mother. Bear teaches us to look within our own sacred dens for wisdom and answers to life's questions. Bear may have healing medicine of all kinds to share with you in the lessons it offers.

How Bear Can Warn Us of Danger

Like many people, Bears can sometimes be too quick to anger and too sure of their own power. While Bears have little to fear, they can forget caution, a necessary response when dealing with many of the two-leggeds today. Do you sometimes throw your sense of caution to the winds? Do you wander into places where you should not go? If so, heed Bear's warning that being unaware of your limits in certain settings can lead to disaster.

Beaver

Behavior and Habitat

Beavers are the engineers of the animal world, altering the environment around them to a degree exceeded only by human activity. The dams they build to ensure their food supply, as well as their safety, can turn a forest stream into a pond or a lake by flooding the land behind the blockage. Once they stop maintaining the dam, for whatever reason, and it gives way, a treeless meadow remains where the pond had replaced the forest.

Beavers are aquatic mammals, the largest of the rodents found in the United States, where they live in northern climates. Adult males can weigh up to 60 pounds. Their fur is waterproof, and their chisel-like front teeth are coated with a hard, dark-yellow enamel that makes them almost unbreakable. Beaver's front paws have claws for digging and working with mud, while their rear feet are webbed, so they swim very well. Their broad, leathery tails serve as rudders for swimming, as support while they stand to gnaw at trees, and as a way to sound an alarm when smacked on the surface of the water.

Beavers are sociable animals who remain faithful to their mates and family. They are also extremely peaceful. Given their claws, large teeth, and broad tail, one would think they could defend themselves in a fight, but it is simply not within their nature to do so. They prefer to deal with potential predators by running away to the safety of the lodge they have constructed within their dam. This living area is deep within the structure but above the waterline, where the Beaver family can stay dry and protected. They seal the roof of their lodge with a thick layer of mud; when this freezes in the winter, it creates an almost impenetrable fortress.

Beavers eat the soft bark of trees. One reason they build dams is to have a deep pool in which to store trees so they will have an easily accessible food cache when winter snows make it hard for them to get around on land. They often dig side channels through which they can float logs downstream to their dam, which is built of trees whose bark they have eaten and trees with inedible bark, held together with rocks and mud. Their structures can become massive and elaborate; one of the largest ever seen measured 2,140 feet long and 4 feet high and was 23 feet thick at the base.

How Beaver's Medicine Gifts Help Us

The medicine of Beaver is the power to build and shape. If Beaver has logged its way into your awareness, it might be saying that it is time for you either to build something new

and secure for yourself, or to repair the leaks in something you have already made. If you need to create something really effective in some area of your life, you would do well to call upon Beaver's gift for industrious design. As a creature of the water, the element associated with emotions, Beaver can remind you to be gentle with yourself as you work hard and to retreat to the security of your lodge when that is necessary.

How Beaver Can Warn Us of Danger

A Beaver out of water—out of balance with its own nature—might stray too far from the safety of its home in search of trees and become an easy meal, especially since it doesn't occur to the little fellow to fight. Are you venturing too far into unfamiliar territory? Are you putting yourself in a position of risk without resources for self-defense? If Beaver has come to you, it may be telling you to stick with the familiar for now. The only time a Beaver should wander off is when its home waters have become too crowded and it needs to make a new pond of its own.

Bee

BEE'S MESSAGE:
Take the time to give and to serve.

BEE'S WARNING:
Don't be needlessly defensive.

Behavior and Habitat

It is estimated that one third of all our crops are pollinated by Bees. There are approximately 25,000 species of Bees worldwide and 3,500 in North America. Of those, only about ten species are what we call Honeybees, who are fascinating creatures. The queen is hatched from the same type of egg as the worker, but she is fed a different diet and raised in a separate chamber by the nurse Bees, causing her to develop into the much larger queen Bee.

Honeybees store honey, which they make from nectar, in a hive of hexagonal chambers. Like squares and triangles, hexagons can be fit together with no wasted space, but the six-sided hexagon is the most efficient way to contain space using the least amount of wax. Honey is consumed by the Bees when nectar is unavailable, and is also a delicious food sought after by many animals. Bees are not aggressive unless provoked, but they will fight to protect their honeycombed homes. When a Bee does sting, it injects toxins that can kill small birds and people with allergies, and the Bee itself will die because part of its abdomen tears away with the stinger.

Honeybees have an interesting way of communicating among themselves, using a complex combination of scents and dancing. The "waggle dance" seems to convey a map to a good food source to the other Bees in the hive. Scientists have found that the Bees are somehow able to accurately communicate the location of the food by telling their hive-mates to keep the sun at a certain angle relative to them as they fly, even taking into account the motion of the sun.

Bees might seem like poor candidates for higher mental functions, such as good memory, but as with most creatures, a closer examination yields surprises. A certain Bumblebee gathers nectar from clusters of monkshood flowers in the Colorado Rockies. These Bees have to visit several flowers on each trip to get a good amount of nectar. They then fly back to the hive to deliver their bounty and repeat the process again and again. Obviously it would be a waste of time for a Bee to return to flowers from which it had already taken nectar. In 482 trips made by one Bee whom observers tracked on a particular day, the Bee duplicated flowers it visited only five times!

How Bee's Medicine Gifts Help Us

The power of Bee is service. Bees serve the many flowers and trees from which they gather nectar by cross-pollinating them. They serve the hive through their building of honey-combs and production of honey. And their honey provides a sweet treat for animals and people. If Bee has buzzed into your awareness, it could be reminding you that, as a part of all existence on the Earth Mother, you need to give back to life as well as receive its gifts.

How Bee Can Warn Us of Danger

Out-of-balance Bees, such as the Africanized Honeybee, attack things that aren't really a threat to them. In so doing, they kill themselves and hurt other creatures unnecessarily. They do this primarily because they have too large a defensive range and try to claim too much territory as theirs. Are you being too protective of your space and hurting others and yourself in the process? If so, you might need to learn the lesson of the balanced Honeybee and become a more harmonious part of the whole.

Bobcat

BOBCAT'S MESSAGE:
Develop your personal power through more independence.

BOBCAT'S WARNING:
Don't violate the boundaries of others.

49

Behavior and Habitat

The Bobcat, also known as the Bay Lynx, shares some characteristics with the Canada Lynx but is smaller and more adaptable than its northern cousin. Both have bobbed tails and tufts on the ends of their pointed ears that are believed to help capture sound, though Bobcat's tufts are less pronounced. Unlike almost all other felines, neither of these cats has an aversion to water and both have been known to jump into water after prey or to elude trackers. Bobcats in captivity will even soak in a pool of water on a hot day.

Both Bobcat and Lynx are solitary animals who hunt primarily at night. Their territory may extend from five to fifty miles across, depending upon the availability of prey. The favorite food of Lynx is the snowshoe hare of the far north. Lynx have adapted to their snowy environment by developing large, heavily furred paws that allow them to travel atop the snow as if on snowshoes.

Bobcats enjoy a greater variety of prey, from birds and bats to rodents, rabbits, and even young deer. They can surprise their prey by pouncing from as far away as ten feet. Bobcats range from Mexico to Canada in desert and forest, growing to a length of three feet and weighing up to 20 pounds. In the wild they can live for around 12 years. Bobcat kittens will stay with their mothers for up to a year to learn how to hunt properly before setting out on their own.

How Bobcat's Medicine Gifts Help Us

The power of Bobcat is independence. Most cats are independent by nature, but this is especially true of Bobcats. They are self-sufficient and seem to enjoy their solitude. Even though there may be over one million of them living in the United States, they are rarely seen by people. Therefore, an encounter with Bobcat is truly a gift and could very well have great meaning for you. If Bobcat has padded its way into your life, it might be saying that you have become too dependent on others and you need to break some bonds that are limiting you. Bobcat is not suggesting that you cut yourself off from others, but that it might be good if you had more of the personal power that comes from being able to meet some of your own needs. If you feel dubious about your ability to handle some situation in your life, ask Bobcat to help you reclaim your power so you can act from a place of strength.

How Bobcat Can Warn Us of Danger

An aspect of Bobcat's independence is its attitude that fences, barns, and chicken coops are surely meant to keep someone *else* out. Bobcats have gotten into trouble by going places where they are not welcome and preying on livestock, which can put them in a perilous position. Are you so free-spirited that you believe warnings are for someone else? Do you overstep your boundaries to get what you want? If so, heed Bobcat's message and know that, while it is good to be independent at times, it can be dangerous when your desire for freedom impinges upon the rights of others.

Buffalo

BUFFALO'S MESSAGE:
Healing is available on all levels.

BUFFALO'S WARNING:
Be more flexible.

Behavior and Habitat

Properly called American Bison, Buffalo can weigh up to 1,200 pounds, although in times past the males sometimes reached almost twice that weight. Buffalo are incredibly hardy creatures who grow thick coats of fur to survive extremely cold winds and deep snow. When the snow is high, they use their massive heads like plows to push the snow out of the way so they can get to the grass below. As the weather warms, they shed their excess fur in clumps, which birds happily use for nesting material. When summer insects start to bite, Buffalo like to roll in dust and mud to make themselves less appetizing. They also have the habit of rubbing themselves on rocks and trees to relieve itching; in so doing, they kill trees by rubbing off their bark.

Buffalo bulls and cows both have horns. When defending against danger, the cows form a protective circle around the calves, and the bulls encircle them all. While this strategy worked well against wolves, it was a poor defense against out-of-balance humans who shot them for their hides and tongues, or sometimes just for sport. One such "mighty" Buffalo hunter was none other than George Armstrong Custer, who, not surprisingly, graduated last in his class at West Point. Several years prior to the Battle of Little Bighorn, Custer was massacring Buffalo on the Plains, when a large bull suddenly turned and charged him and his horse. In defense, Custer fired his gun but missed his mark and shot his horse through the head, killing it instantly, and was unceremoniously dumped on the ground. The Buffalo, perhaps not knowing how to respond to this odd behavior, stopped, turned, and walked away, leaving Custer to his future fate.

There were once three different species of Buffalo in the United States, numbering an estimated 50 million. By the time the wanton slaughter was stopped in 1906, there were only about 800 of the Plains Buffalo left. Their numbers have been increasing steadily; today there are over 200,000 Plains Buffalo, some of whom live wild but most of whom are on ranches where they are raised for food.

How Buffalo's Medicine Gifts Help Us

Buffalo is a bringer of healing medicines. According to legend, White Buffalo Calf Woman brought to the Plains people the gift of the sacred pipe to smoke for healing and communication with Spirit. Buffalo horns are also powerful tools for healing. When Buffalo were near, the people would have food, tools, furs for clothing, and hides for shelters. Buffalo literally gave to the people the gift of life. No part of the animal was wasted, as the giveaway of its life was considered a sacred act. If Buffalo has come to you in a good way, it is bringing you a message that abundance and healing are available to you if you will accept the gifts and honor their source.

How Buffalo Can Warn Us of Danger

What contributed to the near extinction of the Buffalo, apart from the obvious factors of human greed and arrogance, was their highly visible and defensively unmovable nature. While such behavior was not out of place in their natural environment, it did make them exceptionally vulnerable to the European onslaught. Are you being too stubborn about something? Have you become an easy target by being too visible? If so, maybe Buffalo is warning you to become more subtle and circumspect in the ways in which you interact with the world.

Butterfly

BUTTERFLY'S MESSAGE:
The path before you is clear.

BUTTERFLY'S WARNING:
You may be disturbing the natural flow of life.

Behavior and Habitat

There are about 20,000 species of Butterflies worldwide, ranging in size from one eighth of an inch to almost 12 inches across. All begin life as caterpillars feeding on plants until they gain enough mass to form a chrysalis and transform. The emergent Butterfly feeds mostly on flower nectar. Instead of a mouth, the Butterfly has a proboscis, a long straw-like structure through which it drinks nectar and juices. It is interesting to note that many of Butterfly's close cousins in the Moth family, which includes about 140,000 species, do not eat as adults; they will reproduce and die without a single meal!

Some Butterflies also live brief lives. Swallowtails live for only about one month—just enough time to find a mate and perpetuate the species before they cross over to the next world. Others, such as the famous Monarch, can live much longer. These delicate creatures, which weigh about the same

as two rose petals, make an amazing migration of thousands of miles.

Butterfly's senses are very different from ours. Butterflies can't hear, but they can feel sound vibrations. Their taste sensors are located in their feet, so by standing on their food, they can taste it. They have compound eyes with thousands of light-sensing lenses that allow them to see not only a portion of our visible spectrum, but into the ultraviolet as well.

How Butterfly's Medicine Gifts Help Us

Butterfly represents harmonic balance. The wings of these graceful air-dancers are beautifully colored, and patterned to be perfect mirrors of each other. Butterflies spread beauty by pollinating the flowers on which they feed. They represent the element of Air, quickly changing and ever moving. They are messengers of the moment who can take our awareness beyond the mundane. If Butterfly is fluttering by, it might be carrying a message that whatever you were doing or thinking about when it appeared is a worthy target at which to direct your energies at this time in your Earthwalk. Once when Gary was contemplating a decision, "a Butterfly relative landed on my hand and remained there just long enough to send a clear message that the choice I was considering was the right thing for me to do."

How Butterfly Can Warn Us of Danger

Whenever an ecosystem is damaged, Butterflies are usually the first to leave. They are especially sensitive to the harmony of Mother Earth's ways. If Butterfly has come to you in a weak, hurt, or trapped way, perhaps you are being warned that something you are doing is disturbing the natural design of your life. If you can determine what has you off-balance and make that right, you'll be able to dance along in closer rhythm with the beauty all around you that is called life.

Cougar

COUGAR'S MESSAGE:
Move into a leadership role.

COUGAR'S WARNING:
Don't be overly elusive and aloof.

Behavior and Habitat

Cougars are known by different names in the various regions where they are found, the most familiar being Mountain Lion, Puma, and Panther. Their range is from the Yukon to southern South America, mostly throughout the western parts of both continents. Cougars are solitary, elusive, and rarely encountered in the wild.

The bodies of full-grown males can be up to five feet in length, plus another three feet of tail, and they can weigh close to 200 pounds. These big Cats are crepuscular, hunting at dawn and dusk, but they are active at other times as well. They will eat a variety of animals, from a mouse to an elk, but their primary prey is deer. Cougars are great jumpers. They can cover 30 feet in one bound, leap 15 feet vertically to land on a tree branch, and jump even further down to the ground without injury. Mountain Lions do not roar as their cousins in distant Africa do; instead they purr and howl.

A mother Cougar will teach her cubs how to hunt by first bringing them a kill, then bringing small prey back alive so that they can kill it. Her cubs will stay with her for up to two years, and during that time they hone their skills by mock hunting, with the mother chasing after them and gently biting them on their necks by way of instruction. The female is very dangerous if an animal or human gets too close to her cubs. There is a report of someone finding the bodies of a female Cougar and a black bear in a death grip at the bottom of the mountain near her den. Wolves and Cougars have a very competitive relationship, and one has been known to kill the other if it served a need.

How Cougar's Medicine Gifts Help Us

Cougar brings the gift of wise leadership to the people. This medicine is evidenced by their quiet strength and self-assurance, in the careful balance they have with their environment, and in the ways mothers teach their young. Cougar knows when to keep its own counsel and be solitary and deliberate. Cougar also knows when to exercise its authority and is often portrayed in Native stories as a leader of the Council of Animals. If Cougar is bounding toward you, it may be saying that it is time to take charge of a situation and exercise a leadership role. You might find it helpful to seek guidance from Cougar if you are called on to lead or facilitate a group.

How Cougar Can Warn Us of Danger

Cougars can be so unobtrusive that one might forget they are present and unwittingly violate their space. Such intrusion could result in a needless confrontation with Cougar over territory. Do you prefer being in the background to the extent that you might not be noticed or considered until a conflict arises? If you prefer to keep out of the limelight, Cougar could be warning you that while there is comfort in solitude, there could be problems if other people neglect to consider your needs for space and privacy.

Coyote

COYOTE'S MESSAGE:

Pay close attention to a lesson.

COYOTE'S WARNING:

Don't try to avoid paying *close* attention to a lesson.

Behavior and Habitat

Coyotes live in virtually every area of the North American continent and are more numerous today than ever before, largely because of their remarkable adaptability. Their preferred habitat is open grassland and thinly wooded brush, but they can adjust to almost any environment that offers some kind of food. Although they can survive on insects, fruits, and berries, their favorite food is meat, fresh or spoiled. They hunt day or night, working alone to take small rodents and reptiles, and hunting in packs to bring down larger game. Coyotes mate for life, living in underground dens where the family unit is well-protected. When their local population is high, they have fewer pups, but when food is abundant and not many other Coyotes are around, litter size grows.

COYOTE

How Coyote's Medicine Gifts Help Us

In some legends Coyote is portrayed as a trickster, meaning that he likes to put obstacles in our way as we walk along our sacred paths. As such, he is often viewed with hostility or fear. Other stories acknowledge that Coyote is here to teach us about ourselves, like a spiritual mirror, but many imply that he does so in an insensitive, disruptive way. The fact is that often the lessons we most need to learn are the hardest ones and we try to avoid them—this is what makes Coyote's persistence so annoying.

Creator gives everyone a purpose for being on the Earth and wants our spiritual growth in actualizing it to be as gentle as possible. If we're not sure of our purpose or if we forget it, Creator sends us messages, speaking softly to us—a whisper here, a coincidence there, or perhaps a visit from an animal relative. If we are living in the moment, have an open heart, and are paying attention to the world around us, we can receive these communications. But many times we are distracted and don't get the message; or we hear, but push the message from our minds because it is something we don't want to deal with, a lesson we don't want to learn. If one spends too much time trying to ignore the teaching, then a more direct intervention from Spirit may be necessary. Often it is Coyote who is sent as the emissary to remind us that while our well-being is of concern to Creator, our unfolding into who we are meant to be is the real purpose of our Earthwalk.

Coyote is not consciously trying to trick us, but he will make sure that a needed lesson comes back again and again, louder and louder, until we are ready to learn from it and to grow. Our stubborn resistance to moving forward is the reason so many of us seem to repeat patterns in our lives and relationships. And Coyote is a powerful teacher indeed with regard to relationships, because it is when we are in a relationship that we can fool ourselves the most.

If Coyote has trotted into your life, you are being asked to look at something you have been avoiding. Call on Coyote as an ally in negotiating a difficult situation. Or thank him for coming and rescuing you from a trap that you are caught in, or for showing you a way in which you are fooling yourself about something. Coyote is not out there to get us, but to teach us, whether we want to learn or not. The next time you find yourself struggling, and things don't seem to be flowing very smoothly, take a minute and ask what the lesson is. Ask to see where you are blocked. It's a safe bet that if you don't take the time now to examine those things in your life that are being Coyoted a little, soon enough they will get Coyoted a lot.

How Coyote Can Warn Us of Danger

"Will you *please* pay attention?" Coyote might plead with you. And he might ask: "How clearly must your question be answered before you can recognize that Spirit keeps trying to give you the best answer? Do you resist because the information that keeps coming to you is not what you want to hear?" Coyote could be warning you to stop avoiding the truth.

Gary describes this personal experience to help illustrate how Coyote works: "Some years ago when I was looking for land to buy in northern Washington, I read a description that sounded perfect: ten acres with water and old trees, mostly flat, and relatively secluded. In ceremony I had prayed that if this was the right place for me, all would go well and I would be able to find the land and purchase it. I set out with only vague directions to guide me but found the road the property was supposed to be on. However, I could find none of the

property markers the owner had described, and after several hours, I gave up, feeling frustrated and angry. That's when I saw the name of the road for the first time: 'Coyote Trail.' I was so aggravated at that point that I got out of the car, picked up a rock, and hit the sign right in the 'Y' of 'Coyote,' blaming him for my troubles.

"Minutes later, I was on the highway, heading for home, having long before forgotten my prayer that Great Spirit do whatever was best for the land and for my Earthwalk. The very first car that passed me sent a pebble flying up that chipped my windshield. It was at that moment that everything became clear and I laughed and laughed. Obviously, the answer I was being given was: 'No, this is not the right road for you now.' Coyote showed me that, by forgetting my sacred intent and by letting my ego get attached to the idea of the land, I was blinded. I never looked again for that land, and I never fixed that rock chip because, ever after, it made me smile to see it."

Crow

CROW'S MESSAGE:
Seek and share wisdom with others.

CROW'S WARNING:
Let go of your ego for the good of a group.

Behavior and Habitat

Well adapted to diverse environments, Crows are found all across North America. They will eat whatever is available in their habitat—insects, earthworms, small amphibians and snakes, eggs and nestling birds, nuts, vegetables and fruits, clams and mussels, and so on. They will also scavenge in your garbage and eat carrion, and they are not above trying to steal an easy meal, perhaps harassing a fox or other animal into dropping its prey. Whenever they can, young Crows con their parents into feeding them long after they are able to fend for themselves. On occasion, Crows have been observed riding on the backs of foraging pigs, hoping to snatch a mouse that might be unearthed.

Because of their taste for corn and other agricultural crops, Crows have long endured persecution by humans. Like the coyote, Crows are viewed by some as a nuisance and steps are taken to reduce their populations. But also like coyotes, Crows have adapted brilliantly to novel circumstances and have even expanded their range, moving into suburban areas and cities.

Crows are among the most intelligent birds in the world, capable of developing a complex language of sounds with which they communicate to one another. In areas where humans hunt Crows, many of the birds can now recognize a gun, in which case they give a "depart" signal to everyone in the forest. Many Crows are skilled mimics, able to imitate perfectly such sounds as the cackle of a hen and the crowing of a rooster, as well as some words in human speech. They quickly learn to associate noises with events, especially when it comes to the distribution of food; that is to say, they know what it means when they hear us lift the lid off the can of feed corn.

Crows have a complexity in their interactions with each other that humans can only begin to understand. For example, Crows seem to like to play practical jokes. One young Crow was observed hiding in a hollow tree and loudly giving the distress call. The nearby murder of Crows rushed to the sound, ready to assist the one in trouble. Not finding the caller, they flew away. The little Crow repeated this over and over, until finally it popped out of its hiding place and "laughed" at the other Crows. The flock, rather than being angry, burst into a cawing chorus of approval.

How Crow's Medicine Gifts Help Us

Crow brings to us the gift of the council. Crows frequently travel in groups and will make mischief in teams. They can be seen perching in neighboring trees and cawing back and forth. They seem to be deciding on a course of action and who will do what. One of the Crows might then explore something new while the others watch closely to see what happens and to learn from it. If Crow is speaking to you, its message might be to come together in council with others in order to learn from one another and make decisions in a good way. In all of your group interactions, be sure to honor the process of decision making, be it in your family, at your job, or perhaps as a member of a circle that does ceremony. There must be balance and harmony in a group, and this is Crow's specialty.

How Crow Can Warn Us of Danger

Sometimes Crow can be a little too arrogant with its loud caw and its clever ways. When you are working with a group of people, do so honestly and with respect for others. It is okay to be forceful and fiery at times, but once a decision has been made, accept it, even if you don't agree with it. This is council in harmony, which is crucial if a group is to be effective. Crow could be warning you to let go of your need to be right— even if you are—for the good of the whole.

Deer

> ## DEER'S MESSAGE:
> Be more aware of all things in your environment.
>
> ## DEER'S WARNING:
> Don't be overly sensitive.

Behavior and Habitat

The Deer that live in North America are White-tailed, Black-tailed, and Mule Deer. White-tailed Deer are the most abundant hoofed animal in North America. Usually they stay in one general vicinity with which they become very familiar. Mule Deer, who mostly populate the western region of the country, migrate around different altitudes depending on the season and rainfall patterns.

Deer are vegetarians; they eat various grasses, fresh green leaves, and tender tree branches but are also happy to help themselves to a fruit or vegetable treat from someone's garden whenever they can. The only way to keep a garden safe from these athletic animals is to enclose it with a fence at least eight feet high that they cannot jump over.

Only bucks have antlers, which drop off every year in midwinter. They grow new antlers from spring to fall, at which time the males compete for the right to mate with does. As bucks mature, the new antlers that grow back every year become larger, but nutrition is also a major factor affecting antler size. Thus, the healthiest bucks grow the largest antlers and have a distinct advantage in mating. This asset becomes a liability in terms of hunting by humans, however, since large antlers make the most-prized trophies.

Being the prey of every large predator, as well as smaller ones who hunt in packs, Deer are extremely sensitive to their surroundings. Deer can move their ears in any direction without moving their heads and can hear a higher frequency range of sound than humans. At the slightest disturbance or suspicious scent, their awareness is triggered. At the snap of a twig, they will bound off before you know which way they went, running in bursts of up to 45 miles per hour. Deer are always cautious. Even those who visit our backyard and see us every day in the winter while we're putting corn out for them will let us get only so close before they bolt and run back down the hill.

Deer have been observed playing a combination game of tag and hide-and-seek, which no doubt improves their evasion skills. They stalk each other through the forest, sometimes doubling back, overtaking another Deer, and tagging it with a hoof. And on occasion we have watched small groups in our backyard simply racing around in all directions as if every one of them had a bad case of the "crazies."

How Deer's Medicine Gifts Help Us

Deer's medicine gifts are gentleness and sensitivity. Very few people who are in tune with life can see Deer's sweet face and not be moved. Hearts and temperaments soften around this sacred carrier of peace and tranquillity. If Deer has dashed into your awareness, its message may be that you need to be more aware of your surroundings so you won't stray from your path and get lost in the forest. Allow Deer to help you connect to the beings around you and treat them all with the same attitude of loving compassion that Deer engenders.

How Deer Can Warn Us of Danger

Deer's sensitivity can be detrimental in our modern world. Every year approximately 300,000 Deer are killed on the highways by vehicles, and many people also are injured or killed in such accidents. Deer can see extremely well in subdued light, but their heightened senses make car headlights blinding and overwhelming, resulting in the large number of collisions. Are you overly sensitive to unforeseen events that occur in your life? If so, heed the warning of this gentle medicine teacher: Don't get overwhelmed by troubles or surprising turns, so you won't end up on the wrong road.

Dolphin

DOLPHIN'S MESSAGE:

Focus on moving toward unconditional love.

DOLPHIN'S WARNING:

Deal with a troubling emotion.

Behavior and Habitat

There are 32 species of Dolphins in the world's oceans. These aquatic mammals live in schools numbering from 20 to several hundred. They eat a wide variety of fish, and despite the fact that they do have teeth, they tend to swallow meals whole. Like bats, Dolphins use echolocation to find prey.

Dolphins spend a large portion of their day playing, and they will mate all year round. Females give birth to a single calf, often with other Dolphins surrounding her to assist with the birth. They pull the newborn calf out by its tail and lift it to the surface for its first breath. They are all fiercely protective of the young ones in their schools, and they have been known to band together to kill an attacking shark or other predator by repeatedly ramming it at high speeds. Young Dolphins usually spend two to three years close to their mothers. Injured and sick Dolphins are also cared for by others, who support them near the surface so they can breathe. Dolphins have also been known to help members of other species, and accounts of their saving human lives are numerous and well-documented.

Dolphins communicate through a complex language of clicks, whistles, grunts, and body postures. A young Dolphin gets a name in the form of a unique whistle that incorporates elements similar to its mother's name. Dolphins know the names of the others in their school and whistle those names to get their attention. In some scientific studies examining brain-mass ratio as an indicator of intelligence, Dolphins are considered just below humans in terms of intelligence. Other studies of a similar nature rank them above us.

How Dolphin's Medicine Gifts Help Us

Dolphin's gift to us is a model for community in balance. Dolphins live their lives in joyful harmony with each other and with the world that supports them. They play most of the day, talk to each other by name, help one another, make love all the time, don't go to war, and don't pollute their environment. Are they perhaps *more* intelligent than we are? Hmm . . .

Dolphins do seem to have learned the lesson that love is the most important part of life. Some people with mental and physical challenges have shown significant improvements in attitude and aptitude after swimming and playing with Dolphins. This is because our aquatic relatives have a purity of being and a gentleness of spirit that touch our inner nature. Call on Dolphin when you need help achieving a state of unconditional love and acceptance with the other beings in your life.

How Dolphin Can Warn Us of Danger

Dolphins have been known to inexplicably beach themselves in large numbers. When that happens, perhaps they have been following a sick or injured Dolphin in an attempt to render aid. Perhaps they are all sick and are trying not to infect other Dolphins. Maybe they are attempting to communicate something to their land cousins that we have yet to understand. We may never know their reasons. But if Dolphin has come to you through a negative encounter, it could be advising you to look deep inside to see how your own well-being might be threatened if you close yourself off to the love that exists in the world all around you.

Dragonfly

DRAGONFLY'S MESSAGE:
Discover and enhance your innate skills.

DRAGONFLY'S WARNING:
Don't be afraid to alter old patterns.

Behavior and Habitat

Dragonflies have been around for 200 to 300 million years. One Dragonfly fossil that was found had a wingspan of over two feet. Today the largest Dragonfly is found in Costa Rica, with a wingspan of seven inches. There are about 2,500 species in existence today, 400 of which can be found in the United States. The spectacular colors in their transparent wings and stick-like bodies glitter with iridescence on a sunny day.

Despite its large size for a flying insect and its commanding appearance, the Dragonfly poses no threat whatsoever to humans or to our activities. Throughout their lives, however, Dragonflies are a great threat to other insects and a major predator of mosquitoes. As newly hatched nymphs, Dragonflies live on the bottoms of ponds and streams, where they try to satisfy their ravenous appetites by eating the larvae of insects, including mosquitoes—and Dragonflies! When they

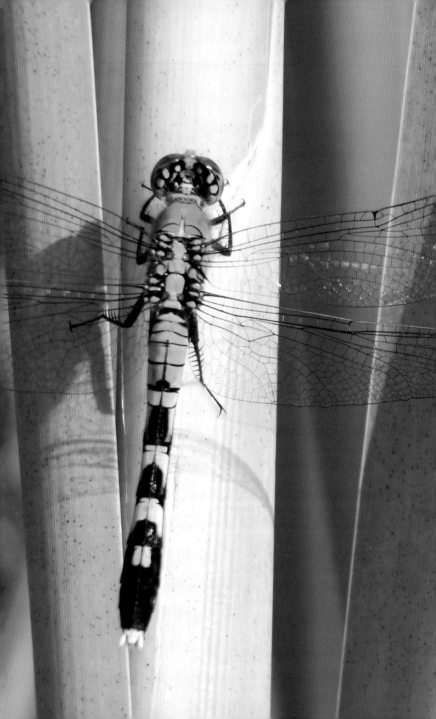

transform into adults, they use their flying skills to track down and catch less-mobile insects, which would be just about all of them.

Dragonflies have amazing flight capabilities: starting, hovering, flying forward and backward, darting up and down, zipping this way and that way. This mastery is made possible by two sets of wings that do not have to beat in unison like those of other four-winged insects. Their front wings can be moving upward while the back ones are going down. All of Dragonfly's legs are located together at the front of its body. They are not designed for walking, though they can be used to grasp a perch. Instead, the Dragonfly uses its six legs to form a basket that catches and holds dinner until it decides to stop moving long enough to eat what it has caught.

How Dragonfly's Medicine Gifts Help Us

The various beings who feed on the bountiful insects of the air have each created a unique way of accomplishing the task, but no bird or insect demonstrates as much magic in flight as the Dragonfly. The strength that Dragonfly brings to the world is skill. They are experts at what they do, and they do it tirelessly. If Dragonfly's aerial dexterity has brought it into your notice, it may be delivering a message that you, too, have innate talents you need to recognize and cultivate. Now is the time to develop your own natural gifts, find joy in all facets of their evolution, and allow your spirit to sparkle.

How Dragonfly Can Warn Us of Danger

We once asked a friend who lives beside a river if she would like to have a Dragonfly magnet to stick on her refrigerator. Without hesitation, she responded, "Oh, no, thank you! I see enough of those buggers all summer when I'm hanging out in the river, and they keep landing on my head because I'm the only land around!"

It is quite possible that there really are just a small number of them who keep returning to use her head as a rock, since Dragonflies tend to establish a fixed route of locations where they fly around to look for food. This can become problematic if the food supply in a frequented area becomes depleted. The fact that you're blessed with skills that support you well now does not mean that it is no longer necessary to learn new things and adapt to changing circumstances so you can grow to your full potential. Learn from Dragonfly that rigid patterns can be limiting, and keep working to gain more knowledge and refine your talents so they can better serve you in the future.

Eagle

EAGLE'S MESSAGE:
You have clear vision.

EAGLE'S WARNING:
Remember to give thanks to all of Creation.

Behavior and Habitat

There are more than 50 species of Eagles inhabiting all major land regions except Antarctica and New Zealand, but the United States is home to only the Bald Eagle and the Golden Eagle. Both of these birds range in size from two to three feet long, with wingspans exceeding six feet. Bald Eagles are primarily fishers and always live near some body of water. The Bald Eagle is not above robbing another bird of its fish by harassing it in flight until the other bird drops its catch. The Golden Eagle is more often seen in forested areas, preferring to feast on rabbits, large rodents, and other birds. Both raptorial birds have extraordinary flying skills, soaring as high as 10,000 feet above the Earth. While diving at prey, the faster Golden Eagle can reach speeds of up to 90 miles per hour.

Eagles seem to choose their mates for love, for they become devoted to one another and will stay together until death. They dedicate themselves to raising their young ones, taking turns carefully incubating the eggs. Their nest is built high in a tree or on a rocky ledge, where it will stay safe from most predators, and is made of many twigs and lined with grass and leaves. Each year the birds add new material to the nest; sometimes a family will use the same nest over many generations. The largest nest ever measured was 20 feet deep and 9 feet across and it weighed well over 1,000 pounds.

All of this is done for the benefit of two or three white eggs that are less than three inches long, and for the Eaglets who hatch and will stay there for as long as three months. The aerie serves as play and training ground, where the

Eaglets will learn to prune their lengthening feathers, grasp objects with their talons, and filet a fish or dissect a rodent. A nestling who is reluctant to fledge from its lofty treetop nursery might need a little coaxing from its parents.

How Eagle's Medicine Gifts Help Us

Golden Eagle flies closer to Creator than any other bird and thus is the Sacred Messenger, carrying our prayers to Creator and returning with gifts and visions for the people. Eagle's keen powers of sight can help us see beyond the ordinary into the Spirit realms. Eagle feathers have long been considered sacred by many Native peoples and are used to adorn medicine objects; they are believed to aid in making the connection when healers need to talk with Great Spirit. If Eagle has blessed you with its presence in some way, you are being given potent gifts of clarity and vision to use for the good of all beings. You can bring light forth out of the darkness.

How Eagle Can Warn Us of Danger

The Sacred Messenger can gently remind us that Creator does not judge us but wants us to keep in our minds and hearts what is important in life. Are you talking with your relations and praying, or are you placing other things ahead of communicating with the Spirits? We will always have busy schedules, but Eagle reminds us that we must also find time to honor the many gifts that we have been given and to give thanks for everything that is dear to us.

Earthworm

Behavior and Habitat

There are approximately 2,500 different kinds of Earthworms. Their segmented bodies vary in length from less than one inch to over ten feet, in the case of a certain species of Australian Earthworm. Without eyes or ears, these creatures are not able to see or hear, but they do possess certain organs that are sensitive to light and touch, enabling them to distinguish differences in light intensity and to feel vibrations in the ground. They also have the chemical senses of taste and smell. Earthworms do not have lungs but instead breathe through their skins.

Earthworms are hermaphroditic, meaning both male and female. They have both sex gonads in separate segments of their bodies. During mating, two Earthworms exchange sperm, which they later use to fertilize their own eggs. Interestingly, some Earthworms have created behavioral patterns and courtship rituals that prevent self-fertilization.

Earthworms eat plant debris and other organic matter in the soil, as well as the soil itself. They tunnel deeply, bringing subsoil closer to the surface and mixing it with topsoil in the process. The benefits of combining and aerating various soil layers are that the soil can hold more water, the bacteria that cause decomposition are able to thrive, and the soil is greatly enriched for the health of plants. Earthworms also deposit a nitrogen-rich material as they move through the soil that is itself an important plant nutrient. In short, everything that

Earthworms do in the natural course of being Earthworms makes soil much more fertile than it would otherwise be. Up to one million Earthworms can dwell within one healthy acre of soil; in a single year, they can bring to the surface more than eighteen tons of earth.

How Earthworm's Medicine Gifts Help Us

Earthworm brings the power of fertility. These life forms play both male and female roles in reproduction and sometimes even have to be careful not to reproduce with themselves! By means of the sacred crawl that they do, Earthworms make fertile ground for plants and, ultimately, for all life. If Earthworm has surfaced near you, you are being asked to determine how you might improve the life-giving fertility of your Earthwalk. Are you enriching the environment around you? Are your thoughts, actions, and emotions positive and life-affirming? Earthworm's advice might be to do what feels natural and nurturing so as to create an environment in which the beings around you can flourish.

How Earthworm Can Warn Us of Danger

When a heavy rain comes, Earthworms crawl to the surface to get out of the water. Water is the element representing emotion. Are you comfortable with strong feelings, or do you head for dry ground when the floods come? Do you struggle to escape from situations that affect you more strongly than seems reasonable? Emotions should not control or overwhelm us, but neither should we hide from our feelings or deny how we feel. If one's life is in balance, emotions flow freely and then are released.

Elk

Behavior and Habitat

It is estimated that ten million Elk lived across a wide swath of the United States before Europeans arrived and reduced the Elk population to less than 100,000 by 1900. Programs designed to increase their numbers in their historic ranges have reintroduced Elk into several states as far east as Pennsylvania. These efforts are proving fairly successful, even though the now-extinct eastern species of Elk is being replaced with its western cousin.

Elk typically weigh from 400 to 700 pounds. Adult bulls with a full set of antlers are a fair match for any animal they might encounter, including a bear. Like Deer, Elk have contests to see who will mate with the does, but unlike Deer, Elk will fight very aggressively and frequently draw blood, or worse.

Bull Elk have a very loud and powerful bugle call that they use to signal their presence and their domination of territory. It can be heard for many miles by female Elk and by male rivals. There is no more impressive a sight than a full-grown Elk, with its winter coat, standing tall and looking majestic. (See "Gary's Encounter with a Reindeer," on page 238.)

Males and females forage together over the winter, separate just before calves are born, and come together again for the autumn rut. Individuals in a herd that is attacked will often bolt in all directions so as to confuse a predator. Elk can run for a very long time, and wolves who prey on Elk will be able to chase down only the weak or the injured. Elk tend to be rather aloof and are not generally seen along roadsides.

In addition to regular teeth, Elk have unique teeth called ivories, which are highly valued by many Native American peoples. The most sought-after ivories tend to show interesting patterns and are often used to adorn women's dresses and powwow regalia. Depending on the tribe, ivories represent fertility or long life. Elk are also commonly known by their Shawnee name "Wapiti," which means "white rump."

How Elk's Medicine Gifts Help Us

Elk shares with us its regal demeanor. It uses the gifts it has been given as part of Great Mystery to full advantage, with a bearing that is a natural projection of its inner self. If you need to be impressive in a situation, it would be good to connect with Elk and learn from it how to make your presence noticed. Elk's medicine can help if you are shy or unsure of yourself. If Elk has strutted into your life, it may be telling you to polish your aura and carry yourself with pride and power generated from within.

How Elk Can Warn Us of Danger

Unfortunately, many different types of people are aware that Elk has power, sometimes to its detriment. For example, the South Koreans buy millions of pounds of Elk antlers and velvet every year to make medicinal tonics and aphrodisiacs. Desire for such products has led to illegal poaching to supply this market for Elk antlers. If Elk has come to you, and you are already well aware of your gifts, it may be warning you that at times it is better to be a little less grand, so as not to become an obvious target.

ELK

F l y

FLY'S MESSAGE:
Now is the time to be persistent.

FLY'S WARNING:
Know when to let something unfold of its own accord.

Behavior and Habitat

There are tens of thousands of species of Flies. They develop through the same basic life cycle of egg, larva (better known to us as the Maggot), pupa, and then adult. A female Fly can lay several hundred eggs at a time, generally in decaying matter. Then, depending on the species, in a few days or weeks those eggs mature into adults that, in a conducive environment, can reproduce in an astoundingly short period of time into millions of Flies. In the case of the common Housefly, the maturing process takes about one week. It takes even less time for the Drosophila, or Fruit Fly, to reach its adult stage, so this is the species often used by geneticists in their experiments, since they are able to study several generations within the space of just a few days.

Adult Flies feed on many substances but prefer decaying materials, including dung. Whatever their diet, Flies must take their food in liquid form. If need be, Flies will regurgitate strong acids and enzymes onto solid food to convert it to liquid, which is then sopped up by the Fly's spongelike mouth. All of this they do quickly, so a Fly landing on your meal should be shooed off at once or it could make your food unpalatable—at least psychologically! Flies can carry and spread many diseases, which is another reason to keep them out of your space.

How Fly's Medicine Gifts Help Us

Fly has the power of persistence. Gary recalls, "Once, while I was deep in thought, trying to make an important decision about whether a path I was following was right for me, I was sitting by a window with a Fly in the room. It was

busy trying to figure a way out through the window, which must be a strange thing to a Fly. When the window is open, they see nothing and can come and go. When it's closed, they see nothing and can't come or go. Anyway, the Fly kept bashing itself against the window for the longest time. I was lost in thought and paying it little mind, but when I finally did, I opened the window and out it flew. It dawned on me at that moment how stubbornly persistent the Fly had been and how it never stopped going up against a seemingly immovable barrier until finally, miraculously, it wasn't there anymore. Fly's lesson helped me make my decision." If Fly has come to you in a meaningful way, it may be saying that you need to keep at something until the way to your future is made clear.

How Fly Can Warn Us of Danger

Persistence in matters of personal growth and discipline is very good. Persistence that becomes annoying to others is not as good—that is one reason the production of flypaper, sprays, and traps is a mega-industry. If you are sometimes tenacious to the point of hurting your own cause, Fly may be warning you that, while this technique might achieve your objectives, it doesn't make you any friends along the way.

FOX

FOX'S MESSAGE:
It's time to try a subtle and clever approach.

FOX'S WARNING:
Don't be too crafty for your own good.

Behavior and Habitat

There are several different types of Foxes with varying colors of fur. They are not very large animals, the biggest weighing around 25 pounds. However, their bushy tails, which can measure two feet, often make them appear larger than they are. Vixens have litters varying from two to ten pups. They are the only canines with some climbing ability, and the very adept Gray Fox can scoot up a tree in cat fashion, holding on with its front legs and pushing with the rear. Fox is satisfied with a wide variety of things to eat, including small mammals, birds, eggs, insects, nuts, and fruit. Near the shore, Foxes eat urchins, shellfish, and if they are hungry enough, even beach flies.

All Foxes exhibit the extreme cleverness and cunning that gave rise to the expression "sly as a Fox." Foxes being pursued by hounds have been known to run across the tops of walls, cross streams diagonally, double back on their trail, venture onto thin ice that won't support the dogs, and even take a ride on the back of sheep in order to break the line of scent.

Foxes are also clever in their play. An observer told of a Fox who truly seemed to be playing with a shrew and enjoying the fun (though the shrew probably would not have called it that). The Fox had just killed and eaten a mouse when it caught another one. It killed that one and stored it away in a food cache, apparently no longer hungry after its first snack. The Fox then caught a shrew, took it to the center of a road, and put it down. The Fox proceeded to jump and yelp and run circles around the shrew, trying to keep it corralled. Several times when the shrew escaped too far from the center, the Fox retrieved it and brought it back to the middle of the road.

After a while, the Fox seemed to tire of the game and the observer expected the Fox to kill the shrew and store it with the mouse, that being common behavior. But the Fox picked up the shrew in its mouth, carried it back to the hole where the Fox had found it, and let it go; the shrew, of course, disappeared immediately. It seemed to the observer that the Fox had had so much fun with the shrew that the Fox just didn't want to kill it.

How Fox's Medicine Gifts Help Us

Fox brings us the gifts of cleverness and subtlety. Foxes have great ability to outwit both predators and prey with intelligence beyond mere instinct. If you find yourself in a situation that calls either for a subtle touch or for slipping out quietly, call on Fox to guide you. If Fox is running circles around you, it may be advising you to stop being so obvious in your actions and to approach things more discreetly.

How Fox Can Warn Us of Danger

Some caution is recommended when you work with Fox's medicine, since its talents for deception and evasiveness have made it a favorite target of hunters with dogs, looking for a challenge. Fox could be warning you that being too crafty or too subtle can sometimes backfire and get you into trouble. If you become too invisible, the result may be that your words are not heard and your ideas are ignored. As in all aspects of life, balance is the key.

Frog

Behavior and Habitat

There are roughly 4,000 species of Frogs living everywhere around the world except Antarctica. The United States is home to about 80 species, varying in size from the small Wood Frog, at less than two inches, to the Bull Frog, whose body (not including extended long legs) can be eight inches long and can weigh one and a half pounds. Frogs have extremely sticky tongues, which they shoot out several inches with great precision to snag a meal that could consist of any type of insect.

Frogs are best known for their singing by lakes, ponds, and streams. In general, only the males croak in pursuit of a mate. Clusters of eggs laid in water hatch into fishlike Tadpoles, which breathe by means of gills. The metamorphosis from

Tadpole to Frog happens when limbs develop, lungs replace gills, and the tail is absorbed. Frogs take in the water they need through their skin, which is a primary reason they are especially sensitive to environmental degradations.

Most Frogs survive the winter by burrowing in soft mud to below the frost line and hibernating, but the Wood Frog has an interesting adaptation. Buried under a pile of leaves, a Wood Frog might appear to be frozen solid in midwinter, when in fact it is only partially frozen. This Frog survives the cold by producing a large quantity of sugary glucose that acts throughout its body like an antifreeze, preventing ice crystals from forming and damaging delicate cells. Meanwhile, its breathing and heartbeat will stop until the spring, when the Wood Frog thaws out and resumes normal activity.

Toads are related to Frogs, but the two families differ in several ways. Frogs are thinner and have longer back legs than Toads, thus enabling Frog to leap and move faster than the sluggish Toad, who hops. Frog's skin tends to be colorful and smooth, while Toad's is often brown with warts that contain poison glands to deter predators. Frogs are found close to water; Toads prefer drier ground and generally hibernate under leaves. Only eighteen species of Toads are found in the United States.

How Frog's Medicine Gifts Help Us

Frog is the caller and cleanser of the emotions, which are often associated with water. In some traditions, Frog is the spirit keeper of the element of Water, singing healing songs to quiet our inner turmoil. Some Amazon tribes could predict the rains based on the songs that Frog was singing. If Frog

jumps into your awareness, look at the emotions you are experiencing at that moment and decide if they are in harmony with the rhythms of nature, or if they need cleansing.

How Frog Can Warn Us of Danger

Many Frogs secrete liquids that coat their skin, making them taste bad to predators. If a predator were to pick such a Frog up in its mouth, it would most likely spit the Frog out quickly. Some of the secretions are even poisonous, and if a predator were too quick for its own good and swallowed one of those Frogs, it would topple over. The poisonous Frogs, including the bright-red Poison-Arrow Frog of the Amazon, are usually colored in distinctive ways to warn predators away prior to an encounter. Unfortunately, their bright colors make these Frogs easily visible to humans, who capture and kill them to extract their poisons. Are you sometimes too defensive? Are questions directed your way perceived as personal attacks? If so, heed Frog's warning that too strong a defense just might become a liability.

Gopher

GOPHER'S MESSAGE:
It's time to gather and save for the future.

GOPHER'S WARNING:
Don't enrich yourself at the expense of others.

Behavior and Habitat

Generally speaking, Pocket Gophers come in two varieties: Eastern and Western, depending on which side of the Rocky Mountains they inhabit. Pocket Gophers are so named because of pockets in their cheeks, in which they carry extra food back to their burrows. They are solitary beings who come together only for mating, living almost their whole lives underground in complex tunnels dug with their sharp front teeth and claws. The burrow system of a single Gopher, who can move a ton of soil in a year, may extend over several hundred feet and result in numerous mounds of excavated dirt.

Gophers range in length from six to twelve inches. They have small eyes and very poor vision and are active primarily at night. They are prey to every carnivore larger than they are and the favorite meal of Gopher snakes. When faced with an attacker in its cavern, the Pocket Gopher can run backward almost as fast as forward, using its tail as an antenna to feel the openings in its passages. It will also fight bravely, though generally to little avail.

The Gopher knows all about putting food by. It does not hibernate during the winter but rather lives off the food that it has stored. Unfortunately for us and for them, Gophers like to gather the same plants we like to grow. This includes vegetables, grains, flowers bulbs, and the bark and roots of trees, especially fruit-bearing ones. Many people with gardens consider these relatives of the squirrel to be a terrible nuisance, since they tunnel under gardens and pull large numbers of plants down into their burrows. Moreover, their excavations create hazards for anyone walking on the ground above them.

How Gopher's Medicine Gifts Help Us

Unlike squirrels, who often cannot find what they cache, Gopher is a true gatherer. Gophers have to live all winter on what they can store during warmer days of greater abundance. If you are trying to save something for the future, you might want to connect with this industrious little being and ask it to teach you some of its tricks. If Gopher has tunneled its way to you, see where in your life you might best focus your attention so as to prepare in an effective way for the future. It is incumbent upon each of us to have the tools, materials, and talents that we might need in case things change, which can happen suddenly and dramatically.

How Gopher Can Warn Us of Danger

Gophers have many conflicts with people who share their dependence on the bounty of the soil. If Gopher is making its presence noticed in your garden or elsewhere in your life, it may be appropriate to look at whether, perhaps unintentionally, you are diminishing something that someone else needs as you attempt to satisfy your own requirements. Part of a balanced Earthwalk is to accept what is being offered to you along your path, but it is important to distinguish between what is truly being offered and what you would like to have that really isn't up for grabs.

Grasshopper

GRASSHOPPER'S MESSAGE:
Honor the wisdom of your elders and ancestors.

GRASSHOPPER'S WARNING:
Don't fall victim to greed.

Behavior and Habitat

Grasshoppers, Crickets, and their relatives have lived on the Earth for approximately 300 million years. Like all insects, they are coldblooded and are more active in warm weather. It is possible to tell the temperature quite accurately by the number of chirps made by the Snowy Tree Cricket, as well as some of the other species.

There are between 10,000 and 20,000 species of this type of insect, depending on whose count one uses, and each species of this multitude has its own unique song. With few exceptions, only the males are able to sing. During courtship, male Grasshoppers take turns singing songs, attempting to outdo each other for the attention of females. If a female is attracted to one of them, she will select the victorious singer as her mate. If no female comes, the competing males will occasionally break out simultaneously into what can best be called a "national anthem" for their species.

How Grasshopper's Medicine Gifts Help Us

The gift our musical relatives bring to us is the power of sound and song. Music in the form of song is an ancient way to alter consciousness and open doorways so that interactions with our relations in the spirit realms can take place. According to a Chippewa–Cree storyteller with whom we spent time, some Native American songs date back at least 20,000 years. Rattling, which sometimes sounds similar to Grasshopper's singing, is also an ancient and effective way to reach the spirit world through music.

If these insect singers have caught your notice with their musical expressions, they may be asking if you are honoring your ancestors and the wisdom of their ways. And are you taking time to hear the rhythms and harmonies within yourself so that you can connect with the songs of the Earth Mother and all who reside upon her? Maybe Grasshopper or Cricket is giving you the gift of a memory, along with a message to take time to listen to the music of the spirits.

How Grasshopper Can Warn Us of Danger

Overcrowding and food shortages can turn some species of normally peaceful Grasshoppers into swarming hordes of dreaded locusts, capable of stripping bare a forest or a farm in the blink of an eye. Instead of Grasshopper green, they turn dark, almost black, so they can absorb more sunlight with which to generate the energy to maintain their frenzy. This frantic behavior will continue until they find a place with enough food to support them all, or when large numbers of them die or are killed through human efforts to control their population.

Are you in a situation where you have to fight for a piece of the pie? Are you someplace that brings out the worst in you? The gifts of Mother Earth are available for everyone if they are sought and honored in a sacred way. Some people disregard the precariousness of life's fragile balance and are taking more than is reasonable and right; they are human locusts. The warning here may be for us all to stop participating in the greedy destruction of the planet and to willingly come into balance with natural forces before the Earth itself acts to limit our numbers.

Horse

HORSE'S MESSAGE:
It's time to move, travel, and be free.

HORSE'S WARNING:
There can be a price for freedom.

Behavior and Habitat

There are approximately 100 different breeds of Horse and Pony, ranging in size from Miniature Horses, at 20 inches tall at the shoulder, to draft Horses, who can weigh one ton and stand 72 inches high. Their life span is generally 20 to 30 years but some have lived considerably longer, the record being 62 years. Horses can sleep either standing up or lying down, and will choose depending on how safe they feel, given that they are prey to large predators. In the wild, the herd is protected by some members who keep watch.

Wild Horses once numbered in the millions, but their lands were taken and they were hunted for domestication and for use in commercial products. Some were inducted into service in World War I. An incomprehensible number of them were killed because they were considered a nuisance by ranchers and farmers seeking to cultivate western lands. There are still a few true Mustangs in parts of nine western states, but for the most part the wild Horse has gone the way of the roaming buffalo herds. While they were still abundant, Horses helped transform a continent. They pulled the wagon trains and helped build the railroads that allowed the West to be taken by the Europeans. And Horses helped turn the Lakota and several other Native nations into the powerful mounted warriors that they became.

Native people quickly realized that they shared with Horse a burning passion for freedom, and many developed an almost magical ability to work with Horses. Instead of "breaking" Horses into submission as cowboys bragged of doing—yielding a Horse that was fearful and broken—Native warriors "gentled" the Horse into cooperation, creating for both human and Horse a trusted friend and companion for life.

How Horse's Medicine Gifts Help Us

Horse is freedom, and it shares with us the power that comes with being free. A Horse gives its rider the safety of speed. Horses gave Native peoples tremendous power to run, fight, send messages, hunt, and move their villages quickly. To steal a Horse was to steal power from another tribe. Some shamans, when traveling to other worlds for knowledge or healing, will do so on a Spirit Horse. If Horse has come racing into your life, it may be saying that it is time to move somewhere, either physically or spiritually. Is there somewhere that you want or need to go for your learning and growth? Horse can help you get there safely.

How Horse Can Warn Us of Danger

Horse could be bringing you a warning message. Before this continent became so populated, the land was well-suited to the feral Mustang, who had adapted itself to live in a very harsh environment. Mustangs thrived, even with limited water, on a diet of coarse grass, sagebrush, and juniper that would not have sustained most Horses. Their need to have freedom in great open spaces, however, quickly made them unsuited to a country whose people seem compelled to control and dominate everything. In your need to be free, are you trying not to play by the rules? Are you pushing boundaries that will cause others to push back? Is your need to go your own way so strong that you can't accept any restrictions, or advice? If so, your free-spiritedness might not necessarily be a bad thing, but heed the lesson of Mustang: There can be a high price to pay for freedom.

Hummingbird

HUMMINGBIRD'S MESSAGE:
Allow the gift of beauty around you to lift your spirit.

HUMMINGBIRD'S WARNING:
It's time to share a gift that you have been given.

120

Behavior and Habitat

There are nearly 20 species of Hummingbirds that spend time in the United States, but, with accidental exceptions, only Ruby-throated Hummingbirds are found in the eastern half of the country, where they multiply in late spring and summer. Often, these mighty little birds cross vast portions of the Gulf of Mexico on a treacherous migration of 1,800 miles between the eastern United States and Central America, where they winter.

Hummingbirds flap their wings at the fantastic rate of 90 beats per second during normal flight, giving them their humming sound. As mating season begins, the male claims a territory, and when an interested female appears, he does a courtship dance, flying back and forth in an arc with wings fluttering at 200 beats per second. The male's involvement is limited to the mating act, after which he goes off to look for other females. The mother lays the eggs, incubates them for the required 16 days, and raises the young by herself.

Hummingbirds have excellent maneuverability in flight. In fact, they have become so aerodynamically adept that they have completely lost the ability to walk and are able to use their weak legs and feet only to grip perches. They are small, but because they expend so much energy in motion, they require large amounts of sugar-rich flower nectar and must consume twice their body weight each day to stay alive. Their diminutive size can be a disadvantage should they fall prey to any of a wide variety of carnivores, sometimes even a frog, a dragonfly, or a large spider. A Hummingbird's brain is over 4 percent of its body weight, the largest proportion in the bird kingdom. It makes them clever enough to remember which flowers they have visited and even how long it takes those flowers to replenish their nectar.

How Hummingbird's Medicine Gifts Help Us

Hummingbird's colors are quite beautiful to our eyes. This is because the iridescent quality of bird feathers is not the result of pigmentation but is dependent on the angle at which light strikes tiny grooves and ridges on their feathers. Like a prism, these structures break the light into its rainbow colors. Hummingbirds' eyes are designed so that they see in the low ultraviolet light spectrum, revealing to them more, and even more amazing, colors than we see. Can you imagine?

Hummingbird brings us the gift of beauty. All of Creator's children are beautiful in their own ways, but Hummingbirds stand out. They are different from every other winged one in their unique flight abilities and feeding habits. While their speed and sound may sometimes startle us, that awakening pulls our attention out of the mundane so that we can acknowledge and appreciate the marvels of Creation. Hummingbird reminds us to give thanks for all the beauty in the world and thanks that we are a part of it.

How Hummingbird Can Warn Us of Danger

In Victorian times, showcases of stuffed Hummingbirds could be found in people's homes, and until such practices were made illegal, their feathers were widely used to decorate clothing and hats. People tried to capture the beauty of these flying wonders, to trap it and keep it for themselves. If Hummingbird has come to you, it may be humming a warning in your ear that you cannot keep a gift from Creator just for

yourself; it needs to be shared. Is there some gift that you can give to the people that you are holding back? If so, do as the Hummingbird, and let your own gift of beauty shine.

J a y

JAY'S MESSAGE:
Understand your needs and goals more clearly.

JAY'S WARNING:
Don't use your power to overwhelm others.

Behavior and Habitat

There are around 30 species of Jays in North America, the three most common of which are the Blue Jay, Stellar's Jay, and Scrub Jay. They are related to crows and magpies and, like them, are extremely intelligent and vocal. They learn fast and have been known to rob campers of food and potential nesting materials, sometimes traveling in teams to make their mischief. Captive Jays have used strips of newspaper to rake food pellets in from outside their cages.

Jays talk to one another using a complex language that some other animals have come to understand. If a human hunter stalking prey annoys a Jay, the bird sounds an alarm that other creatures, including deer, can interpret as a warning to flee. Blue Jays also mimic the calls of hawks in order to trick rivals away from food or nest. A Jay skilled enough to make the shriek of a hawk believable will soon find that it has the bird feeder all to itself.

Jays eat mostly seeds, nuts, fruit, and insects, and we know that Blue Jays, at least, have a passion for peanuts. Jays are not above robbing eggs from a neighboring nest now and again, and in fact they sometimes usurp the whole nest of another bird instead of building one themselves. They tend to bury acorns for winter retrieval but, like squirrels, can't find them all, thus helping to revitalize oak forests.

Jays are very territorial. They don't like predatory intruders and often harass cats, dogs, and even people who approach their nesting areas. We once watched a cat stalk to the base of a tree where Steller's Jay was sitting no more than three feet up. Instead of flying away, however, the Jay started squawking at the cat, who was so startled by the Jay's role reversal that he slinked away. The Jay kept voicing its disapproval long after the cat had gone.

How Jay's Medicine Gifts Help Us

Jay has a power of presence. Jays are sure of themselves and assume it is their right to act as they will. If Jay is fussing at you, its advice may be to walk your path with more certainty and confidence. When you are in tune with the purpose of your Earthwalk, you will know who you are and what you need, and you will be able to move toward your destination in a clear and determined way.

How Jay Can Warn Us of Danger

Jays have earned a reputation for being greedy and domineering. They can be bullies at backyard feeders. If enough of them decide to claim your diner as their own, they will prevent other birds from visiting and might even yell at you if you are late with their breakfast! This behavior can be shortsighted, however, since it can make people less willing to put food out for just this one greedy kind of bird. Do you have a confidence that knows no bounds? Do you use your voice and your words to intimidate or to make false hawk calls? If so, Jay's warning to you might be that while it is good to be confident, it is not good to use force of personality to dominate and control others. You may sometimes get what you want, but at what cost?

Jellyfish

JELLYFISH'S MESSAGE:
Move with the natural flow of things.

JELLYFISH'S WARNING:
It's time to stop drifting around.

Behavior and Habitat

Jellyfish live in warm seas around the globe. There are many different species, some living deep in the oceans where few beings can survive. The most commonly encountered Jellyfish, however, float along on the surface, where the water helps to support their gelatinous bodies, which are over 90 percent water. They lack a skeletal structure or outer shell, so they are delicate and easily damaged. If removed from the water, they collapse and die. Some Jellyfish are quite tiny, unlike the fairly common Portuguese Man-of-War, whose body can be from three to fourteen inches across, with an "umbrella" rising up to six inches out of the water. Its stinging tentacles dangle below the surface of the water for up to 50 feet.

Jellyfish have no brain, heart, or bones, but rather a simple neural system that can respond to prey and other

128

stimuli. When they sense prey in the form of plankton or small fish, muscular stinging cells within their tentacles shoot out barbs and inject toxins. These cells then contract to bring the prey into the main body, where another type of cell digests it. Jellyfish reproduce asexually by creating floating polyps that

bud into little duplicates of the original; this explains why they are sometimes found drifting in colonies. Jellyfish can move somewhat by squirting out a stream of water, but for the most part their movement is determined by where the ocean currents take them. During warmer seasons, they float poleward, and during cooler months, they drift toward the Equator.

How Jellyfish's Medicine Gifts Help Us

The gift that Jellyfish brings to us is acceptance. For their meals, Jellyfish have to take what the bounty of the seas will bring to them. They are dependent on the currents of the ocean and the directions of the winds to move them in the ways they need to go. Even with no brain, they are a very successful life form, having been around in roughly the same design for hundreds of millions of years. If Jellyfish has drifted into your life, it may be advising you to stop struggling so hard to go in a direction that you think is correct. If you let go of your preconceived idea of the right path to be on and move in greater harmony with the natural currents of your life, Spirit will take you where you need to go and provide for you along the way.

How Jellyfish Can Warn Us of Danger

As in all things, we need to seek a balance of the elements. Jellyfish could instead be warning you that perhaps you spend too much time drifting and not enough time actively crossing the currents in a way that will actually get you somewhere. Even Jellyfish can move when they need to.

Lizard

Behavior and Habitat

Out of 3,000 species of Lizards in North America, only about 115 species live north of the Mexican border. These include many different kinds of Horned Lizards, Skinks, Desert Iguanas, and Geckos. A few Lizards are scattered throughout the continental United States, but many more are found only in the desert Southwest. Native species range in size from pencil-thin Legless Lizards to the only venomous Lizard, the Gila Monster, whose thick, heavy body can measure up to 24 inches in length.

There is some variation among members of the Lizard family, but most Lizards share many of the same characteristics. All are coldblooded reptiles, requiring warm temperatures to make them active. Unlike the Desert Iguana, who is often seen out in the midday sun when temperatures exceed 100 degrees, most Lizards prefer to spend the day buried under loose soil or hidden in the shade of rocky outcrops. Most hunt at night for insects, spiders, scorpions, and other small creatures. All have dry, scaly skin that may be smooth or spiny. A few species of Lizards bear live young but most lay eggs.

Lizards can move at amazingly fast speeds—some at more than 15 miles per hour—over short distances. Geckos can run up trees and walls as easily as over ground because they have tiny hooks on the undersides of their toes that catch in the slightest roughness, even in a pane of glass. Lizards rely primarily on speed, camouflage, or hiding to escape the many predators who try to make a meal of them.

Another escape mechanism that most Lizards can call on in an emergency is their ability to voluntarily break off their own tails, using the muscles that surround a particularly weak vertebra. The writhing tail is left behind to distract the predator, while the Lizard darts away. Lizards can perform this magic trick only once, however, since the replacement tail they grow is made of cartilage with no breakaway vertebrae.

How Lizard's Medicine Gifts Help Us

The power of Lizard lies in its ability to save itself from danger by leaving a part of itself behind. If Lizard has scurried past you, it may be suggesting that now is the time for you to shed something that has been an integral part of your life, because it now endangers you in some way. The danger may be at any level—physical, emotional, mental, or spiritual. Have you smoked for a long time? Is your marriage of many years now suffocating you? Is the job you thought was providing security really destroying your creativity? Are old beliefs killing your spirit and making you unhappy? Remember that Lizard leaves its tail behind to save its life, but soon it grows a new one.

How Lizard Can Warn Us of Danger

Lizard would have us exercise caution before we initiate major change. Remember that Lizard can discard its tail only once. Its new one is different from the original, and it won't break away. So make your decision wisely. You may have to live with it for a long time as it follows you around.

Mole

MOLE'S MESSAGE:
Look below the surface for knowledge and guidance.

MOLE'S WARNING:
Re-examine your preconceived notions.

Behavior and Habitat

There are several species of Moles found in the United States, varying in length from three to nine inches. All are virtually sightless and live most of their lives underground. They often establish their dens, which they line with grasses for the comfort of their young, deep under a big rock or tree stump for security and protection from the cold. The Shrew Mole is a most curious creature in that it can stay awake for no more than eighteen minutes before falling asleep again, but then sleeps for only eight minutes or so at a time.

Moles are considered by some people to be pests, but in reality, no subterranean mammal exists who is more helpful to the gardener. With their extremely high metabolism, Moles live to eat. In the course of its lifetime, a single Mole will eat thousands of cutworms, wireworms, and other depredatory insects by consuming its own weight on a daily basis. Moles have pointed snouts and powerful front legs with which they move soil, and they can burrow as far as 75 yards in a single night in their search for food. Their presence can be detected as small moving mounds of earth, popping up as they tunnel along just below the surface.

How Mole's Medicine Gifts Help Us

The gift that Mole brings is the power to skillfully move and explore beyond boundaries. In some Native traditions, Mole brought hidden knowledge to the people and was the first shaman among the animals. Moles are at home in the dark and can move beneath the earth's surface with remarkable speed. Mole's medicine is to help us see and unearth what is hidden deep within our minds and our hearts that keeps us from being happy and experiencing a strong and balanced Earthwalk. If Mole is in your yard, you are being asked to evaluate honestly what is serving you well and what is working against you.

How Mole Can Warn Us of Danger

Many Moles have been killed by humans because of the unfounded belief that they eat potatoes and other underground crops. While Moles might rearrange plants as they move dirt in their search for dinner, their elimination of pests and aeration of the soil provide benefits far greater than any harm they do. Nonetheless, they continue to be destroyed. If Mole has burrowed into your life, it may be suggesting that something you believe to be true may in fact be the opposite of truth. Mole can remind us to see things as they really are.

Interestingly, Moles are notoriously intolerant of others of their own species and will fight one another to the death with their razor-sharp teeth. The fact that they suffer intolerance by humans, yet practice the same behavior against one another, only reinforces the warning that we should let go of prejudice, lest it result in persecution or self-destruction.

Moose

MOOSE'S MESSAGE:
Do something spontaneous.

MOOSE'S WARNING:
Be more reliable.

Behavior and Habitat

Moose are the largest of the Deer species. Adult male Moose can stand seven feet tall, weigh more than 1,500 pounds, and sport antlers six feet across. Moose graze on the soft twigs of willow, birch, spruce, and alder trees; the word "moose," in fact, comes from the Algonquin people, who called this creature "mooswa," which means "twig-eater." Moose also eat grass and moss, but with their long legs and short necks, they must get down on their knees to reach such foods. Moose like water and sometimes will stand in a pond or lake to feed on aquatic plants. They are excellent swimmers and can go for miles at a time.

Moose tend to be solitary creatures, though mothers are extremely protective of their calves—usually one, but twins and triplets are possible. Males bellow very loudly during

138

mating season and can be heard up to three miles away. When they hear a Moose cow answer, they run to her, prepared to battle anything in their way. Park rangers and campers caught suddenly in the path of a Moose on its way to mate have had to take refuge in trees. There are even tales of male Moose attacking trains during rut.

How Moose's Medicine Gifts Help Us

The quality that Moose teaches us about is unpredictability. Moose can run away quickly when it sees you; Moose can just stand there and ignore you; or Moose can take offense at your presence and maul you. Moose can dash out of the way of your car or lope along for miles in front of it as you drive. When we lived in the woods of northern Idaho, we heard about several Moose encounters. One involved a driver who honked his horn at a Moose blocking the road. The Moose took offense at that (or thought it was a funny-looking male Moose) and proceeded to pound the car into such a state that the man had to be pried out of the back floorboard. If Moose has tramped into your life, its message may be that it is time to do something differently. If you find that you are in a pattern that drains your energy and deadens your spirit, you might seek to connect with the energies of Moose to add some spontaneity to your life.

How Moose Can Warn Us of Danger

Moose's message could be a warning to you. People shy away from Moose because there is no foretelling what its actions will be at any given moment. Does your behavior tend to be inconsistent and erratic? Do you sometimes explode in anger that is inappropriate, or express other emotions that are out of proportion to the situation? If so, Moose might be suggesting that you would do well to change your unpredictable ways so that those around you don't have to keep their distance with a wary eye.

Mosquito

Behavior and Habitat

There are approximately 2,700 species of Mosquitoes, and they are found virtually everywhere in the world. Only the female Mosquito requires blood as part of her diet. The male drinks plant juices and is quite harmless except for the role he plays in the reproduction of more females. A single female can lay over 200 eggs at a time in any source of standing water, even something as small as a discarded soda can with a little rainwater in the bottom. If it should happen that the water in which the eggs are laid dries up before they can hatch, the eggs might well survive for as long as five years until more water provides a new environment for hatching.

The female finds her victims by sensing slight increases in the levels of heat and humidity created by breathing, as well as by the carbon dioxide emitted. She then heads upwind until she finds the source of the fluctuations, touches down, and hopes she's found food. Worldwide, diseases transmitted by Mosquitoes are responsible for millions of deaths every year.

How Mosquito's Medicine Gifts Help Us

Mosquito offers us the dubious gift of distraction. If Mosquito has decided to get your attention by bringing its message through an annoying itch, you can react blindly with distress and imbalance, or you can acknowledge that Mosquitoes, too, have a place in the Sacred Circle of Life. If you choose the latter approach, you will be able to come to terms with the simple reality that they share the Earth with us.

Gary recounts: "During a time that I spent on the Earth building my connection with the natural world, a few

Mosquitoes (it seemed like thousands) evidently decided that I was the source of a good meal. I had some choices at that point. I could stop what I was doing and leave the area. I could start swatting, which would be a terrible distraction from my intended task. Or I could see them as a means by which to measure my determination and focus. I chose the last option and used a method that a teacher of mine had once recommended. His suggestion was to make peace with the Mosquito nation and feel no anger toward them, since they were simply doing what Mosquitoes do. By so doing, he believed, their bites wouldn't itch or even leave a mark. (Even my teacher didn't say they would actually stop biting!) I followed his advice as best I could, realizing that Creator has given life to the Mosquitoes just as to me and that I was not so wise as to be able to say they did not belong. With a light heart, I accomplished what I had gone out on the land to do, and the next day, there was not a single sign of a bite."

How Mosquito Can Warn Us of Danger

Mosquitoes make people itch, they spread disease, and generally speaking, everybody hates them. Have they no redeeming qualities? Besides providing food for many insect-eating creatures, Mosquito's best service is perhaps to warn us two-leggeds to be mindful of our own behavior. Do you nag and nip at others to get them to notice that you are around and have needs? Is your style such that people sometimes just wish you would buzz off? If Mosquito has landed on you, it could be warning you to be a little less demanding of other people's energy.

Mouse

MOUSE'S MESSAGE:
Find contentment in what you have been given.

MOUSE'S WARNING:
Look beyond surface illusions.

Behavior and Habitat

There are approximately 1,100 species of Mice world-wide, and they are all extremely successful and prolific. This is because the estrus of a female Mouse can last for six to twelve hours, in which time she can mate from dozens to hundreds of times with different males. Mice multiply at a prodigious rate and will continually gnaw on just about anything to keep their teeth—which are constantly growing—short and sharp. When Mice get inside a structure—be it a factory, a storage facility, a grocery store, or your home—they can be very destructive. They are able to slip through openings you didn't even know were there, and once they are inside the walls of a house, it is possible for them to damage electrical wiring, such that a fire could result. Mice are evasive; in a typical country field there may be thousands of them, but walking through it you probably won't see even one.

On Gough Island in the southern Atlantic Ocean, more than 20 species of sea birds use this isolated and protected locale as a breeding ground. There were no mammalian predators on the island until Mice arrived on ships in the 1800s. The Mice quickly developed a taste for bird chicks, and with plenty to eat, they soon evolved to two or three times their original size. They have also learned to hunt cooperatively and, by working together as a team, they can kill a three-foot-tall Albatross chick. It is estimated that they kill over one million birds each year on this island. On the plus side, virtually every carnivorous creature the world over eats Mice, and by virtue of their prolific breeding, they are an extremely important link in Creation's food chain.

How Mouse's Medicine Gifts Help Us

If Mice have visited you (and they never come alone) in one of the endearing ways they are presented to us when we were children, our numerous little relatives may be reminding you to look carefully at the things that are right in front of you. Even though Mouse's sight is not especially good, its other senses are very acute, and it can find bounty in even the least and smallest things around it. Perhaps you have been fixated on a goal that you think might satisfy you or make you happy in some way. But if you look more closely at what you are seeking, you just might discover that what you already have is better than you realized. Mouse's medicine can teach us that what we have been blessed with may be all that we really need.

How Mouse Can Warn Us of Danger

If your Mouse encounter is more of an unpleasant one, it may offer a clue that all is not as it seems. These small mammals have somehow been elevated to a frightening level of popularity. Mickey Mouse is a worldwide, billion-dollar industry; Mighty Mouse was a television hero for many; Mouse's image appears on everything from greeting cards to children's pajamas. Although Mice are highly destructive to the places they invade—every year they destroy hundreds of millions of dollars' worth of crops, grains, and other property—they have somehow become a symbol of cuteness, fun, and play. If Mouse is squeaking at you, it may be warning you that you need to pierce through illusion so you can see the way things really are.

Otter

> **OTTER'S MESSAGE:**
> It's time to play, laugh, and have fun.
>
> **OTTER'S WARNING:**
> Devote more time to necessary tasks.

Behavior and Habitat

There are two kinds of Otters: Sea Otters and River Otters. Sea Otters live along the Pacific Coast from southern California into Alaska. They weigh between 30 and 100 pounds, the males being much larger than the females. Sea Otters enjoy a smorgasbord of different foods from the sea, which they eat off their chests while floating on their backs. Often they will use a rock to open difficult items such as clams. They are among the few animals who use tools, sometimes keeping a favorite one stored on the ocean floor for regular use. When they have finished eating, they roll in the water to clean themselves.

Sea Otters survive the cold of the sea thanks to very thick fur (they have approximately 800 million hairs) and a high metabolic rate. They often keep their front paws, which lack

fur, out of the water when they are floating on their backs so their paws remain dry and warm. Sea Otters are good mothers, and their young remain with them proportionally longer than do the offspring of most animals. Young Otters are very buoyant, and while they cannot yet dive or even swim, neither will they sink. When the mother dives for food, she will anchor her young one on the surface with long strands of kelp.

River Otters weigh 20 to 30 pounds and measure three to four feet from nose to tip of tail. They live near fresh water all across the United States and Canada, but will leave an area if the waterways get too polluted or crowded. The River Otter often makes its den out of one that has been abandoned by another animal, or it might use a natural, protected enclosure like a hollow log. Generally, the den will have two entrances, one under the water and one higher up that will stay dry. This gives the clever Otter two ways to get in and out of its den, while at the same time providing good ventilation.

In a delightful nature special on PBS called "The Otters of Yellowstone," the subjects play for the photographers for most of the hour—and the worst thing that happens to anyone is a nip on the nose of a Coyote who erred in stalking an Otter. Otters seem to make a game out of everything and to enjoy every minute of their lives. Even while traveling somewhere, the Otters of Yellowstone would run for a few feet, then glide on the slippery snow, then run, then glide, repeat. And as the narrator pointed out, Otters are either "on" (that is, in constant, hyperactive motion) or they are "off" (that is, asleep).

River Otters will also fashion slides in mud or snow on the banks of rivers and then spend endless hours sliding down, running back up, and doing it again. There is no scientific rationale for this behavior, so the best explanation is that the activity is a form of recreation. Sea Otters play as well, and can be seen chasing each other, leaping in the waves, and engaging in what looks like a game of tag. After watching the behavior and interaction of Otters on film, in zoos, and wild in the river below our house, we consider it altogether plausible that they just like to have fun!

How Otter's Medicine Gifts Help Us

Lots of animals play in certain circumstances, especially when they're young and bursting with energy. After all, life for all beings is to be enjoyed, not just survived. But it is the Otter who has elevated play to an art form, giving us the gift of laughter. Otters are joyful, happy creatures who celebrate life by playing together. As we watch them, we are reminded to smile, an important life skill that isn't taught in too many places. It is our (admittedly biased) opinion at Dancing Otter that Otters are the epitome of cuteness. So we like Richard Bach's analogy, from his book *Illusions*, regarding our true nature as humans: "We are game-playing, fun-having creatures, we are the otters of the universe." If Otter is asking you to dance, its message might be that your life could benefit from a little more laughter and lightness.

How Otter Can Warn Us of Danger

Otter could be warning you that you are not taking seriously certain aspects of your life that need a little care. Otter's time for play comes only after it has tended to its needs and those of its family. Are you perhaps not devoting enough time to things that require your attention? Is this perhaps because some of those necessary tasks seem like non-fun? If so, you might want to follow Otter's example and look for ways to make even the unpleasant more enjoyable; that is to say, seek happiness in everything you do. Can you imagine a world in which everyone's aim is happiness? Can you imagine a world in which people really live as Otters do?

Owl

OWL

> **Owl's Message:**
> Change is coming.
>
> **Owl's Warning:**
> Don't be afraid of transition.

Behavior and Habitat

There are about 150 species of Owls in the world, about 20 of which live within the United States. They vary in size from the six-inch Elf Owl to the two-foot-long Great Horned Owl. Owls are mostly nocturnal, and they will eat everything from fruits and insects to rodents and other birds. Owls conceal themselves extremely well when they are sleeping during the day, but if crows and jays discover one, they will group together to drive it away.

Owls have many abilities that set them apart from all other birds. They have a greater range of motion in their necks than any other animal with a spinal column. They turn their heads to glance around rather than their eyes, which do not move. Their night vision is so powerful that some Owls can see prey when the light is equivalent to a candle burning nearly half a mile away! Owl's acute powers of vision are matched only by its preternatural sense of hearing. In studies of Owls placed in totally light-free rooms, the Owls were able to locate a mouse by sound alone.

Also, their wings are extremely soft and thick, with fuzzy edges, allowing them to fly almost silently so they can swoop down on unsuspecting prey. In addition to silent flight, haunting hoots, and uncanny abilities to see and hear in the dark, Owl's aura of mystery is further enhanced by its tendency to inhabit abandoned houses and dark church towers.

How Owl's Medicine Gifts Help Us

The Night Eagle is a messenger from the shadowy realm of darkness and a guide through all of the mysteries found therein. If Owl has oriented itself on you, you can be certain that some aspect of your life is going to change, possibly in a big way. Change is often something that people fear, being so closely related to the unknown. Owl, as a harbinger of change about to happen, sometimes gets fear transferred to it. Consequently, some people have come to believe that Owl makes itself known only when something is about to die. Rather than a physical death, the change could just as well mean saying goodbye to some part of yourself that is not serving you or to an old way of life that is now over. Change can be welcome and transformational.

Sherry tells of her introduction to the sweat-lodge ceremony at a Native gathering many years ago: "Purely by fortunate coincidence, I signed up to be in a sweat lodge with someone who became an important teacher for me later in my life. I went into the lodge not really knowing what to

expect and feeling fearful of the unknown, but I emerged who-knows-how-much later believing that my spirit had truly been transformed. I picked up a stone in the shape of an arrow; it was pointing west. The next thing that happened was my move west to Washington, meeting Gary, falling into friendship, then love, now being here—a place where my spirit is the happiest it's ever been. Transformation can be a splendid thing. With all the change that followed quickly in my life right after that evening in the sweat lodge, I'd be willing to bet there was an Owl right above me in the treetops."

How Owl Can Warn Us of Danger

Whether Owl is bringing you a message that you welcome or a warning that you dread depends greatly on how you perceive the nature of change itself. Are you willing to alter circumstances in your life so that you can receive the lessons you need for your spiritual growth, or do you resist any change, even if it is in your best interest? Owl, with its spectral senses, can be your trusted guide through the dark tunnel of transition to the light shining at the other end.

Pigeon

> **PIGEON'S MESSAGE:**
> Set a goal and trust yourself to get there.
>
> **PIGEON'S WARNING:**
> Give back to that which nurtures you.

Behavior and Habitat

Originally, Pigeons lived on the wild cliff faces of European and Asian coastlines. Today, the Pigeon, or Rock Dove, is known to city dwellers everywhere, and its cousin, the Mourning Dove, is found in more open habitats all across the country. Pigeons can fly for 600 miles in one day, and can travel in bursts of speed of up to 60 miles per hour—or in the case of some specially bred racing Pigeons, over 90 miles per hour! Pigeons reproduce throughout the year, even in winter, and can raise four or five broods annually. The female usually lays two white eggs, and both parents take turns keeping them warm. Males usually stay on the nest during the day and the females at night.

Homing Pigeons find their way back to their roosts, it is believed, by orienting on the Earth's magnetic field with the aid of tiny bits of magnetically sensitive material located in their heads and necks. For hundreds of years, Pigeons were trained by the Chinese to deliver messages, and until the invention of the telephone, they carried money exchange rates between banks within China. Early navigators took Pigeons to sea in the hope that if they became lost, the Pigeon would show them the direction to the nearest landmass. Pigeons have been used extensively for delivering messages in times of war. During a siege of Paris in the Franco-Prussian War of 1870–1871, balloons were released from Paris carrying homing Pigeons, which French sympathizers then used to relay information back into the besieged city. It is estimated that approximately 115,000 official dispatches reached Paris through the blockade due to the efforts of the pigeons.

The Passenger Pigeon, swift and graceful in flight, was once the most common species of bird in North America. During their migration, it was possible to see flocks that were a mile wide and 300 miles long. Some estimates claim that there were as many as five billion Passenger Pigeons when the Europeans arrived on this continent. Once people discovered their many uses, however, the species went from being among the most abundant birds in the world to complete extinction, with Martha, the last one, dying in captivity in 1914 at the age of 29. The history of the frenzied demise of the Passenger Pigeon in a remarkably short span of about 50 years is horrific and reflects very poorly on the human species.

How Pigeon's Medicine Gifts Help Us

No matter where Pigeon ends up or how it gets there, it knows the way home. Pigeons do not get lost because they

are in tune with the natural ways of the Earth and are always aware of their destination. If Pigeon has homed in on you, its message may be that you should keep your sights and sensitivities clearly set on where you want and need to be, and start moving. Even if you don't know exactly how to get there, by following your inner guidance you can find your way along your path.

How Pigeon Can Warn Us of Danger

As we learn from the Passenger Pigeon, nothing in life is guaranteed. A situation or a resource that you thought was secure could disappear in a flash. Therefore, it is important that we treat everything with respect and honor so that it will all remain for the generations that follow. Are you honoring the gifts that you have been given? Do you give back to your benefactors so that they, too, can stay strong?

Porcupine

> ## PORCUPINE'S MESSAGE:
> Ensure that your boundaries are respected.
>
> ## PORCUPINE'S WARNING:
> Be wary of hazards.

Behavior and Habitat

Porcupines cannot move fast at all, but they have very little to run from. Their bodies are quite well-protected by the 30,000 quills they can raise to create a security shield. A Porcupine will actively defend itself by swishing its tail and backing toward an aggressor, so that the barbed ends of the quills are facing in the direction of its foe. Porcupines cannot shoot their quills when threatened, but the quills do come out easily, attaching themselves to whatever touches them. Once embedded in the skin of a would-be predator that gets too close, the quills swell from moisture and warmth. They are shaped in such a way that they work their way in deeper, often causing a fatal infection. A Porcupine can kill a bear or a cougar in this way. A dog that gets quilled will probably need to be anesthetized before the quills can be removed. Some dogs become so obsessed with this unfathomable opponent that they insist upon pursuing them and get quilled time after time—unfortunately for the dogs and for the owners paying the vet bills!

Porcupines are excellent climbers, able to walk up trees almost as fast as they walk on land. In warm weather they wander around in search of favorite grasses, leaves, dandelions, clover, and other wildflowers. Porcupines can swim, so water lilies and other aquatic plants are also part of their diet. In winter they make do with bark and evergreen needles. Females give birth to one to four babies, who are born with very soft quills that harden within a few days. By the age of two months, most Porcupines are ready to live on their own.

Occasionally a Porcupine will fall prey to an Owl or a Bobcat. Its most dangerous enemy by far, however, is the fisher, a large member of the weasel family, who is able to slip underneath a Porcupine and flip it over on its back, exposing its soft underside to the fisher's attack.

How Porcupine's Medicine Gifts Help Us

Porcupine's medicine gift is the power to reflect aggression back to its source. As often as Porcupine is attacked is how often it will defend, simply by virtue of its design. How hard an animal strikes Porcupine is how deeply the quills will be embedded. Unlike Armadillo, who keeps safe but is innocuous, Porcupine stays safe yet is dangerous. Many times in life, someone or something is trying to take advantage of us and we often do not know how to respond. If you find yourself under attack on some level—be it physical, emotional, mental, or spiritual—look to Porcupine for help in turning the hostility back on itself. If Porcupine comes lumbering toward you, take its presence to mean that something could be trying to slip in to get at you. If that is the case, you need to find a way to teach the intruder to respect your boundaries and send it on its way.

How Porcupine Can Warn Us of Danger

Porcupine is not unassailable. Very much like Achilles, who could not be harmed except through his heel, Porcupines have a soft underside and they can be killed by a skillful predator. They remind us that everyone is vulnerable in some way, so don't let your ego make you feel invincible. You may be confident about a person, place, or situation, but be aware that the only constant is change. If Porcupine has appeared and you are feeling safe and secure, it may be warning you to watch out for what's around the next corner so that you don't get flipped upside down.

Rabbit

RABBIT'S MESSAGE:
It's time to confront and overcome a fear.

RABBIT'S WARNING:
Feelings need not control us.

Behavior and Habitat

There are two dozen species of Cottontail Rabbits in the United States, all with similar characteristics. They are quite timid, preferring not to venture very far from safety. Rabbits browse, often at night, on grasses, herbs, and clover, and are fond of garden fare such as peas and lettuce. In winter, their diet becomes coarser and consists of the inner bark of saplings and shrubs, along with any leftover leaves and fruit. During the day, Cottontails tend to remain hidden in vegetation. They have excellent hearing and a very wide field of vision so they can be aware of anything sneaking up on them. If they do sense a predator, they will first try to freeze to avoid detection. If that doesn't work, they flee by running in a zigzag pattern, sometimes reaching speeds of up to 18 miles per hour.

In summer, a pair of Cottontails may produce three litters with three to seven young in each. The babies grow remarkably fast and in two weeks they are ready to leave the nest. They stay with their mother for only another week or so, while they learn what to eat and how to hide. At three weeks of age, a Bunny is off on its own. Unlike the elaborate warrens built by the European Rabbits in Richard Adams' marvelous epic, *Watership Down*, Cottontails shelter in the vacated burrows of other animals or just in shallow depressions amid the brambles. Rabbits provide a perfect illustration of Nature's balance. Their rapid rate of reproduction is countered by the fact that almost every predatory bird, mammal, and reptile looks for Rabbit as a potential meal.

How Rabbit's Medicine Gifts Help Us

Rabbits are afraid of almost everything—and justifiably so. The gifts Rabbit offers us two-leggeds are lessons about

fear. If Rabbit has hopped into your life, it may want you to examine the fears that you hold, especially those deep, reflexive, and often irrational fears that hold you back from achieving your full spiritual potential. Do you keep dashing for the safety of your old patterns every time something new or challenging presents itself? Is the safety of the familiar, even if it is ultimately wrong for you, more comforting than the possibility of something new, and perhaps better?

Sometimes we can bring what we fear most down upon our own heads. There is a story that one day Rabbit saw Eagle circling overhead and yelled up to him, "Eagle, please don't eat me!" Eagle happened not to hear Rabbit, so Rabbit yelled much louder, *"Eagle, please don't eat me!"* Then Eagle noticed Rabbit, and promptly ate him. Fear can control you to the point of causing you to do foolish things. Learn from Rabbit what not to do, and overcome your fears by facing them in a rational way so as to promote your spiritual growth.

How Rabbit Can Warn Us of Danger

Through its timidity, Rabbit also teaches us to be gentle with ourselves. People tend to dislike the fearful parts of both themselves and other people, but virtually everyone likes Rabbit. We need to look upon our own fearful side with the same compassion we have for Rabbit. Accept that it is part of human nature to feel fear at times, but also believe that our fears need not paralyze our growth and movement. Fear is just a feeling, and how we choose to act, or to not act, upon our feelings is one of our greatest freedoms.

Raccoon

RACCOON'S MESSAGE:
Examine your surroundings for a gift.

RACCOON'S WARNING:
Keep to your own affairs.

Behavior and Habitat

There are seven species of Raccoons in North America, but no related species are found in Europe. The average weight of an adult male is around 20 pounds. Raccoons can be solitary, but they also may travel in small groups of one or two families. Although generally not aggressive, they can be tough fighters if attacked. They are slow runners by animal standards, but they like water and are excellent swimmers, easily crossing rivers and lakes, catching the occasional fish when they can. They seek habitats that offer a good source of water, as well as trees for safe refuge. Raccoons are expert climbers, being one of the few mammals who can descend vertical tree trunks headfirst. On warm days, one might be seen resting high in a tree, occasionally appropriating the nest of a hawk or crow.

Usually Raccoons are nocturnal, preferring to spend their days sleeping in hollow trees, rock crevices, or ground dens. They are very opportunistic feeders; they will forage for fruits, vegetables, and birdseed, hunt small animals in your backyard, and, of course, knock over your trash cans. They have been known to raid a house or a farm if food is scarce. In late fall, their fur begins to thicken into a heavy coat, and they begin eating as much as they can find in preparation for winter's leaner times. They might have to spend weeks in their dens without food, but they do not hibernate. Studies have shown Raccoons to be very clever; they were able to open complex locks using their highly developed sense of touch, and they could remember for long periods of time where and how they got treats.

How Raccoon's Medicine Gifts Help Us

Raccoons share their gift of curiosity with us. They will explore and examine a myriad of places and situations for potential food and fun—but mostly food. They will leave no stone unturned in their search for an easy meal. Sherry once awoke to tapping sounds on her window and sat up to find herself eye to eye with a Raccoon perched on the stone wall beside the house. The Raccoon did not scurry off, but looked in as if to say, "Might you have a tasty snack that you could part with?" When Sherry took to leaving food on the porch for it, the Raccoon returned nightly. If Raccoon has come into your awareness, you are being asked to examine your surroundings more carefully and with an inquisitive mind. Perhaps you have overlooked something that could be of benefit to you.

How Raccoon Can Warn Us of Danger

The negative side of curiosity, of course, is that it can get you into trouble if you are prying into the wrong places. According to a Native story, Raccoon got his mask by sticking his nose somewhere it didn't belong and it consequently got burnt. Are you, too, exploring places or becoming involved in situations where you really might not belong? Are you looking for an easy payoff when it might be that hard work is the best way to achieve your goals? If Raccoon taps at your window, only you can determine from your life's circumstances if it is advising you to be more, or perhaps less, curious.

Rat

RAT'S MESSAGE:
Decisions can have many unexpected outcomes.

RAT'S WARNING:
Don't be greedy and wasteful.

Behavior and Habitat

Norway Rats are the species that commonly live among people, destroying property and spreading disease. These creatures would probably not be nearly as prevalent as they are, however, if it were not for humans. Our living habits have provided them with food and shelter, and we have eliminated many of their natural predators. Norway Rats are highly adaptable and have become ubiquitous. While they prefer to live near human habitation or in agricultural fields, they are also at home in forests, deserts, and grasslands.

Rats are ravenous creatures, eating a quarter to a third of their body weight every day. In Europe some years ago, hungry Rats infested a bird sanctuary and ate, among other things, every single bird. They will gnaw on anything to keep their teeth trimmed since, as with most rodents, their teeth are always growing. When food is abundant, Norway Rats produce multiple litters of babies, up to a dozen a year in ideal locations. They are highly social beings and are very intelligent. Rats produce a wide variety of vocalizations, many of which occur during social interactions, such as sparring or grooming.

Despite their name, Norway Rats are not from Europe, having actually originated in central and eastern Asia, including China. Other notable kinds of Rats include Pack Rats, who are famous for collecting things. Pack Rats have been known to strip a sealed cabin in the woods of everything they could carry. There are also the infamous Black Rats, who carried the fleas infected with the bacterium that led to the Black Plague. You may be familiar with the fact that by the time of the Plague, few cats remained on many European streets because fear that cats served witches had led to their mass slaughter in years prior.

How Rat's Medicine Gifts Help Us

If Rat has made itself known to you, it may be trying to encourage you to be alert to unintended consequences of decisions you make. For example, in earlier times world exploration, travel, and trade seemed like good ideas, but many hazards came along with the adventures. One was that Rats managed to successfully colonize the whole world and diminished the populations of many native creatures in the process. Are you doing something that seems like a good idea but really might not be, either for those around you or for the environment? Rat may be asking you to examine what you are about to do in order to see who or what might hitch a ride on your good intentions.

How Rat Can Warn Us of Danger

Rats are very successful animals, just as humans are, and for many of the same reasons. Rat reflects back to us our own capacity for greed. Both species are guilty of taking so much that others' needs are denied. Wanting no competition for food, Rats have dispossessed many other small animals of their homes. Rats will sometimes overeat and regurgitate rather than let any food get by. They exemplify humankind's selfish drives, which are making life on this planet more and more tenuous. If Rat has gnawed its way into your life, it could hold a warning that you are taking more than your share. Are you like so many other humans and the Rats, participating in wasteful consumption?

RAT

Raven

RAVEN'S MESSAGE:
Mystery and magic are headed your way.

RAVEN'S WARNING:
Ground yourself more in the needs of daily life.

176

Behavior and Habitat

Ravens are closely related to crows but are larger, have deeper voices, and are more solitary than their crow cousins, who often assemble in large, raucous flocks. Ravens measure about 25 inches from tail to beak, which makes them the largest songbird in North America. They once inhabited all regions of the Northern Hemisphere, but due to persecution by superstitious people who believed they were portents of evil, there are large areas where they are no longer found.

Although their favorite food is carrion, Ravens sometimes prey on rabbits, rodents, and the nestlings of other birds. They also eat bird eggs, insects, worms, and grains. Ravens have been known to join together to skillfully hunt down game too large for a single bird. They can live in cold northern climates because they do well feeding on animals who don't survive the harsh winters. Ravens build elaborate nests high on cliffs and in treetops and prefer to keep their distance from human habitation.

Ravens are masters of flight, on an acrobatic par with falcons and hawks. Their aerial skills are most on display during the breeding season, when mating rituals include elaborate sky dances, chases, dives, and rolls. Ravens are also clearly among the most intelligent of all birds; in various scientific tests, they have proven themselves capable of using tools and solving problems. They are especially clever mimics and can learn some human words.

How Raven's Medicine Gifts Help Us

Raven brings to the people the gift of mystery. All of Creation is truly a mystery (hence the use of the term "Great

RAVEN

Mystery" as one of the ways of referring to Creation and the Creator), and no animal personifies this better than Raven. Because of their color and their preference for eating dead things, Ravens have long been associated with the mysteries of the unknown, including death. They are coal-black, a color associated with the night, the dark, and all of the fears that reside there.

There are many stories in Native cultures about the mystery and magic of this elusive black bird. Shamans know the power of an unexpected piercing sound in altering consciousness. Ravens exert this power, emitting, as they do, a variety of sounds, some quite sharp and startling. Considered messengers from the other side, Ravens are also associated with psychic abilities, and their feathers are sometimes used to aid clairvoyance. If Raven has flown into your life, you can be sure that something unusual will be happening, something coming out of the Void from the Great Mystery. While you can't fully prepare for the unknown, it is good to meet Raven not with fear, but rather with a mind open to appreciating its magic.

How Raven Can Warn Us of Danger

Raven could be warning you that you are focused too much on the mysterious and the ethereal and not enough on the practical matters of life. There is a time for everything—a time to plant, a time to harvest and gather, and a time for doing ceremony and traveling to other planes of existence. Raven's arrival at your door could bring a message that you are directing your attention toward the wrong place at the wrong time.

Red-tailed Hawk

> **RED-TAILED HAWK'S MESSAGE:**
> Bring passion and energy into your life.
>
> **RED-TAILED HAWK'S WARNING:**
> Don't be possessive and controlling.

Behavior and Habitat

There are roughly 20 species of Hawks living in diverse environments across all of North America. Even skilled bird watchers cannot always confidently identify which one is which, since the patterns and coloring of their feathers vary greatly depending on the season of the year and the season in the bird's life.

One Hawk that does stand out from all the rest is the Red-tailed Hawk. They are the most populous Hawk in the United States, and easily the most recognizable. There are several variants of color in this species; most, but not all, have the visible fiery-red tail. They are very quick, skillful flyers

and are often seen riding air thermals over fields, looking for prey. They prefer, though, to hunt from an elevated perch from which they are able to take off and accelerate rapidly to strike. Red-tailed Hawks eat rabbits, rodents, snakes, frogs, fish, lizards, and even other birds when they can catch them. They seem to be especially fond of rattlesnake meat and will risk the snake's deadly venom to acquire this treat.

Pairs of Red-tailed Hawks mate for life. At the start of breeding season, the pair will go through a spectacular sequence of aerial acrobatics, flying in large circles and gaining great height. Then the male plunges into a deep dive, only to fly high and do it again. Later the birds may grab hold of one another with their talons and fall spiraling toward Earth. A mated pair will occupy the same nest year after year unless the nest is gone or usurped by a more formidable bird. They are considered by many to be the complement of the great horned owl, as they share the same ranges and will sometimes share nests by using them at alternating times of the year. Red-tailed Hawks are called Red Eagles by the Hopi, who give them almost as much ritual significance as true eagles.

How Red-tailed Hawk's Medicine Gifts Help Us

As the complement of owl, the night eagle associated with the Moon, the Red-tailed Hawk has a special connection with the Sun. Red-tailed Hawks are fiery and explosive like the Sun, and they bring these qualities to the people. These birds display various shades of red, like a hot, raging fire. If Red-tailed Hawk is circling above you, it may be saying that you need to embrace the power of your inner fire and come alive with energy and passion for life. If you are clearly aware of what you were thinking or doing when Hawk showed itself to you, look to that as a possible place to ignite your inner blaze.

How Red-tailed Hawk Can Warn Us of Danger

For a long time, Red-tailed Hawks were shot because of an erroneous belief that they ate poultry and were a nuisance to farmers. Misinformed people became so anxious about protecting their livestock that they were willing to kill these magnificent beings rather than find another solution, or perhaps even share. Is there something in your life that you are possessive about and are trying to keep, possibly at the expense of others? Possessiveness is stifling, to yourself and to the person or thing you are focusing on. If Red-tailed Hawk has appeared to you, its advice might be to share a gift you have been given so as to keep the flame of your spirit aglow.

Salmon

SALMON'S MESSAGE:
Stop procrastinating and get moving.

SALMON'S WARNING:
Be wary of an addiction.

Behavior and Habitat

Most fish in the world are either freshwater or saltwater denizens. This is not true of Salmon, who reside in both waters at various stages of their lives. Eggs are laid and hatched in a freshwater stream or pond, and when the fish are old enough, they migrate out to sea. There are several different types of Salmon in North America, all but one of which originate on the Pacific Coast.

When the time comes for them to reproduce, Salmon seem programmed to return to the stream in which they hatched in order to spawn. They are able to do this, even if they have been away from it for as long as six or seven years, by using their amazingly acute sense of smell. At the end of their migration journeys, which can total several thousand miles, a Salmon can locate that one stream it's looking for based on its unique odor. Testing has revealed that a Salmon is able to detect one drop of water from its home stream mixed in with 250 gallons of seawater.

Why Salmon must go back for the purpose of reproduction to the exact place they were hatched is not fully understood, but the impulse is clearly overpowering. Many will encounter obstacles, such as 12-foot waterfalls they will have to jump up and hydroelectric turbines they will have to maneuver around. Salmon will also have to squirm past bears, eagles, and other predators, including people fishing for them, in order to reach their home waters. Despite all of these hurdles, they keep swimming and jumping. And in the end, although the one Atlantic species of Salmon can survive to spawn again, all of the Pacific Salmon will die soon after spawning.

How Salmon's Medicine Gifts Help Us

Salmon bring us the gift of determination. Their drive to reach their place of origin is remarkable. They rarely eat during the trip home, sustaining themselves with reserves of body fat while growing thinner and thinner. Nothing is of interest to them but getting to where they must go. If this sacred swimmer has wiggled into your awareness, it may be telling you that now is the time for you to put all distractions aside and accomplish something that is important to you. Often it is all too easy not to do the things that are so necessary for our growth. Salmon may be saying that the time for procrastination has passed and you must now focus your efforts on achieving a desired or necessary end.

How Salmon Can Warn Us of Danger

If you are a workaholic or are addictively attached to some activity or pursuit, Salmon might be warning you that your compulsive behavior could lead you into the rough waters of suffering and sacrifice. Sometimes it may seem necessary to head toward something with single-minded determination, but we must first be certain that reaching that goal is worth the price we might have to pay.

Seagull

DANCING OTTERS AND CLEVER COYOTES

SEAGULL'S MESSAGE:
Live with more attention to the present.

SEAGULL'S WARNING:
Don't shirk your responsibilities.

Behavior and Habitat

There are more than twenty American species of Seagulls, ranging in length from 11 to 30 inches. Seagulls are excellent flyers and can position their bodies at just the right angle to float in midair, seemingly motionless, by catching wind currents with perfect timing and precision. Webbed feet enable them to paddle around in the water, where they try to steal fish from pelicans. Seagulls are able to drink saltwater because they have a special gland that eliminates extra salt.

Seagulls are still found mostly along coastlines, living by the water near seaports, where they fish for their dinner and scavenge beaches and harbors, helping to keep them clean in the process. But because they will eat just about anything they can digest, some Gulls now live further inland, where they feast on the steady source of food and garbage generated by human excess. They are so comfortable accepting our handouts that many have even moved into crowded urban areas. In agricultural regions, Gulls benefit growers by eating mice who feed on crops. In the mid-1800s, huge flocks of California Gulls saved crops in Utah by feeding on the millions of locusts threatening to wipe out the food supply there. The state marked the event by erecting a monument in their honor.

How Seagull's Medicine Gifts Help Us

Seagulls are relaxed and easygoing in their pursuits, and they bring us the gift of their carefree attitude. When several Seagulls find a fish or some other food, the one who gets there first gets to eat it; they usually don't fight over dinner, though they are quite vocal and will squabble. Seagulls are very casual about how they build their nests, creating a disorganized mess out of sticks, vegetation, and garbage. If Seagull has glided into your life, its message may be to live in the present moment with a more lighthearted attitude.

You might do well to relax your tendency to plan everything out and think everything through. After all, our plans don't turn out as we expect most of the time, and our worst fears usually don't materialize.

How Seagull Can Warn Us of Danger

If you rarely think (much less plan) ahead, Seagull might have a different message for you. Having a carefree nature and living in the moment can be positive, as long as you accept and can manage your responsibilities. Native American people often consider how something done today will affect several generations to follow. So, while needlessly worrying about the future does no good, thinking about and planning for it are important. A warning from Seagull could be to remember that when you commit to something and others are depending on you, it is generally not in anyone's best interest if you suddenly decide to fly off and be free. It is good to temper lightheartedness with responsibility and to know when each behavior is appropriate. Seagull would advise you to find a balance between the two.

Shark

SHARK'S MESSAGE:
Defend yourself in a strong and sure way.

SHARK'S WARNING:
Don't use fear as a tool.

Behavior and Habitat

There are about 375 species of Sharks in the world, ranging in size from the tiny Spined Pygmy Shark, at eight inches, to the massive Whale Shark, at 60 feet in length. The Whale Shark, a harmless filter feeder, is the world's largest fish. Some Sharks, including Blue Sharks, migrate over great distances in the North Atlantic on journeys of up to 2,000 miles. Some species of Sharks must swim constantly because they can breathe oxygen only when water is passing through their gills; others can breathe while still. Remora fish sometimes swim with a Shark, doing their best to keep the Shark's body free of parasites.

Of the many species of Sharks, only ten or twelve are considered dangerous to people. On average, there are fewer than 20 Shark attacks and less than one fatality each year in the United States. The odds of being struck by lightning are far greater than of being killed by a Shark. Nevertheless, Sharks are stereotypically viewed as mindless eating machines. They do have incredibly sensitive noses that can smell one drop of blood in 50 million times as much water, and they can feel the pressure waves made by a struggling fish from far away. While it is true that much of their brainpower is devoted to operating their elaborate sensory systems, Sharks can be trained to perform simple tasks, such as ringing a bell for a meal and distinguishing certain objects from others in the water.

How Shark's Medicine Gifts Help Us

Sharks inspire greater terror in us than their actual danger warrants because they exude the power of the predator. Throughout our history, human beings have been both prey and predator. We have ancestral memory of the fear that predators arouse in us, as well as the courage that is required to overcome it. Perhaps you are in a situation where you have attracted people and events that are now pushing you in directions that are contrary to the way your currents are flowing. When you need the fortitude to frighten away or devour something negative in your life, you might seek help in the medicine of Shark. But you would do well to consider Coyote's teachings at this time, too, and make sure you understand what lesson you will be learning, lest you drive away something that could very well come back again, bigger and bolder than ever.

How Shark Can Warn Us of Danger

Shark might also be sending a warning by pointing out that others often respond very badly toward us if we instill fear in them, even if we pose no real threat. Though Sharks kill an average of fewer than ten people a year around the whole world, humans have killed millions of them. Do you try to control situations by keeping others afraid of you? This could mean anything from threatening someone else's job to yelling at your dog. If Shark is banging on your boat, it might be to warn you that using fear to deal with others can have severe repercussions.

Skunk

> ## Skunk's Message:
> Listen to your intuition.
>
> ## Skunk's Warning:
> Expand the range of your vision.

Behavior and Habitat

There are four species of Skunks that reside in the United States, including Striped Skunks and Spotted Skunks. These clever and adaptable animals live everywhere in this country but avoid dense forests, where the range of their spray would be curtailed. Skunks are relatively slow-moving and spend most of the daylight hours underground. They dig their own dens but will also take over the abandoned homes of other ground-burrowing animals, such as foxes and marmots. Skunks eat mostly insects, but will also consume frogs, fish, eggs, small animals, and snakes. They are quite beneficial to have around since they eat cutworms, mice, and other pests that are far more destructive than they are. Owls pose the greatest threat to Skunk because owls are awesome night predators with a very poor sense of smell, making them less susceptible to Skunk's malodorous defense mechanism.

Skunks are not aggressive and will try to avoid a confrontation, but when a fight is inevitable, they face the threat head on. They are eschewed because of their potent chemical defense, but they use their spray only as a last resort. If Skunk feels threatened, it first raises its tail and stamps its front paws. If that doesn't scare off the intruder, Skunk hisses and turns around, presenting its tail. If the threatening animal still doesn't move away, it gets sprayed. While the spray does smell overpoweringly awful, its stronger effect is that it burns the eyes and temporarily blocks vision. Therefore, Skunks always aim for the face. They can accurately aim and squirt their noxious liquid as far as ten feet, as well as change the size and shape of the stream.

How Skunk's Medicine Gifts Help Us

What Skunk teaches us is how to comprehend a warning. Many times in life, our instincts can sense trouble ahead, but our minds get in the way and block us from hearing this inner wisdom. By watching Skunk and heeding its message, we can perhaps relearn how to honor that part of ourselves that, like Skunk, gives us many warnings before an actual problem or disaster occurs. If Skunk's scent has wafted your way, it could be your intuition trying to get your attention and perhaps even signaling imminent danger.

How Skunk Can Warn Us of Danger

A Skunk out of balance with its own nature will sometimes take to living in the bushes near heavily populated places. A number of Skunks took up residence in a hedge at a harness-horse racetrack in New York that Gary used to frequent. They were peaceful enough, and one could get quite close to them, but officials at the track eventually decided that the track was not a good place for Skunks and they were ousted. Skunk's warning may be that, as you go about your life, peacefully maintaining your home and making your living, you may be out of touch with the bigger picture around you. This seems to be true of the vast numbers of people who are unaware that the impending Earth Changes will make the world very different and will alter many systems that support life as we know it. If Skunk has come to you, it could be bringing the message that your reality is not as secure as you would like to think.

Snake

SNAKE'S MESSAGE:
It is time to move to a higher spiritual level.

SNAKE'S WARNING:
Break out of stagnating patterns.

Behavior and Habitat

Anywhere on Earth that it is warm for at least part of the year, a Snake Sister or Brother has made a home—on land, in water, in the desert, or in the forest. Snakes come in many different sizes and exhibit a variety of interesting habits. Some Snakes, such as the 13-foot-long Cobra and the 20-foot-long Python, lives singly except when mating, whereas others, including the 25-inch-long Adder, can live in dens of up to 30.

Different species hunt in different ways: by poisoning their prey, constricting it, or simply snatching it quickly and downing it whole. Most Snakes have dislocatable jaws, meaning they are not fused together like ours. This feature allows them to eat things that are bigger than their heads. Only poisonous Snakes have fangs, which are hollow tubes similar to hypodermic needles, designed to inject venom.

Snakes are constantly flicking their tongues out to "smell" the air. This activates a chemical sensing organ located in the roof of the mouth; when the tongue is retracted, whatever it sampled in the air is sensed. As a Snake grows, it periodically sheds its skin. During this time, the normally clear protective plate over its eyes becomes cloudy and Snake's vision is temporarily impaired. In contrast to our 33 vertebrae, a Snake can have between 100 and 400 vertebrae making up its spinal column. This type of spine gives Snakes unparalleled flexibility and range of motion.

How Snake's Medicine Gifts Help Us

In many cultures over thousands of years, Snake has been a symbol of life energy and sexuality. The Druids of Europe, many East Indian and Asian cultures, the Mongols, some of the Polynesian peoples, the Native Americans, and the Aztecs all saw Snake as a symbol of power in some way. In East Indian yogic traditions, the Kundalini, or life force, is represented by a Snake rising up through the spine. The way Snake sheds its skin as it grows is an apt analogy for how we shed old ways and habits as we evolve into higher spiritual beings. As in any animal encounter, if Snake has slithered onto your path, note the condition in which it has appeared. If it is a healthy, vibrant Snake, its presence may be an affirmation that your spiritual growth is positive and balanced. If your encounter is with a young Snake, or even an egg, perhaps you are being prompted to recognize a good beginning that you have already made and move it forward.

SNAKE

How Snake Can Warn Us of Danger

If Snake has appeared to you hurt or even dead, it is a warning that you need to begin circulating your life energies now, in whatever way feels right to you. You could meditate, exercise, explore the outdoors, do ceremony, enjoy a good love partner, practice martial arts, make pottery—whatever helps get your life energy flowing in a positive manner. No matter how weak, confused, or lost we become during our Earthwalk, Snake will be close by to remind us that we can shed old ways and begin anew on our path.

Spider

SPIDER'S MESSAGE:
Establish strong patterns in your life to maintain balance.

SPIDER'S WARNING:
You may be doing the right things but in the wrong place.

Behavior and Habitat

There are more than 30,000 species of Spiders, so designated because they all have eight legs and they all spin silk. They live everywhere in the world, even atop Mount Everest and in Antarctica. They all have fangs for seizing prey, and most use their fangs to inject venom into their prey to paralyze it. There are very few Spiders, of which the infamous Black Widow is one, whose venom is potent enough to harm a human. Even the formidable-looking Tarantula, whose body length can grow to nearly four inches, can give us no more than a bee sting's worth of toxin. Some people may not be fond of Spiders, but entomologists believe that without them the Earth would be completely overrun with insects.

All Spiders have spinnerets and can produce silk, but not all of them weave the intricate, net-like webs with which they

are often associated. For example, the well-known Trapdoor Spider uses its silk to construct a camouflaged floor of dirt and webbing under which it hides. It then pops up through its hinged "trap door" and, with lightning-quick reflexes, snatches unsuspecting insects that wander by. Another, the Bolas Spider, spins one long strand of silk, adds a glue-like ball to the end of it, and like a fisherman casting for trout, swings it at prey flying by. The Jumping Spider, so named because it likes to pounce on its prey, uses its silk as a safety line attached to its home so it can easily return after its acrobatic attacks. Spiders recycle their silk and will often eat an old web when they are done with it before spinning a new one.

How Spider's Medicine Gifts Help Us

Many stories exist about Grandmother Spider, the Weaver. In some Native legends, she is said to have brought the people the gift of fire, carrying it from the other side of the world on her back in a basket made of webs that she wove. In other myths, her webs bind all things together and form the foundation of the Earth. Still other stories speak of Spider as the weaver of the threads of life. Spider's medicine can show you how the patterns of your life are interwoven. If Spider has crawled into your awareness, it is a reminder that a person's Earthwalk should be like a web: balanced, even, cohesive, and made according to the unique design that Creator has given each of us to follow. Learn from the Weaver where your life has gaps and snags, and rebuild healthier and stronger patterns in your life.

How Spider Can Warn Us of Danger

Even with their beautiful webs and their relative lack of aggression toward people, Spiders are seldom welcome houseguests. Using our special "bug cup," we routinely escort our eight-legged visitors back to the outside world, but many people do not treat them so gently. If Spider has dropped down on your head, it could be warning you that you may not be in the best place with regard to some aspect of your life. The first part of creating a balanced and healthy web is to pick the proper place to build it. An unhappy Spider encounter could be a sign that even though you are doing things correctly, you may need to be doing them elsewhere.

Squirrel

Behavior and Habitat

There are roughly 350 species of Squirrels around the world, of which ten reside in North America. When nuts and seeds are available, Squirrels eat a wide variety of them, with a single individual burying as many as 10,000 prior to winter. Because they cannot begin to remember where they stored so much food for winter harvest and tend to locate it primarily by scent, Squirrels will often break the shells of nuts with their teeth and then lick them or rub them on their faces to add extra scent before hiding them away. Even so, they fail to retrieve much of their cache, leaving in the ground many seeds and nuts that will grow into trees, thereby contributing to the eco-balance of their woodland habitat. In other seasons, Squirrels will also eat fruits, berries, birds' eggs, leaves, mushrooms, and insects. They are very enterprising in their search for food and clever enough to find a way around almost any obstacle blocking them from a meal, which has resulted in an industry specializing in Squirrel-baffling equipment.

Squirrels are the trapeze artists of the animal kingdom. Their treetop acrobatic feats are unrivaled; little Red Squirrels sometimes jump a hundred feet between trees. It is possible for a Squirrel to fall for hundreds of feet and be unharmed. This is so because their long bushy tails help to slow their fall. In addition to acting as a parachute, Squirrel's tail serves as a rudder for balance, an umbrella during the wet season, a blanket for warmth, and a flag to alert their fellows of danger. Squirrels chase each other for exercise and during courtship, and they have even been observed playing a form of hide-and-seek with each other around tree trunks. They also play with pine cones, pushing them back and forth to each other.

Ground Squirrels hibernate during the winter, sometimes for as long as six months in very cold climates. Tree Squirrels do not hibernate but will sleep for days during the coldest parts of the year. Although Squirrels are solitary by nature, they will sometimes share a nest in order to conserve body heat. As soon as the weather warms, though, the guests depart.

How Squirrel's Medicine Gifts Help Us

Squirrel embodies the quality of trust. Few other wild animals are willing to interact so readily with people. Where Gary lived in New York, trees growing in backyards were full of Squirrels. They had little fear of people or pets, and they would take peanuts from a human hand. Although this practice is probably not advisable, as it can make the animals too acclimated to people or might result in an accidental nip to a finger, it does show us that trusting others can sometimes yield rewards. If Squirrel has scampered into your life, it may be suggesting that you need to let down some of your defenses and trust that the universe will provide something in return that will be of benefit.

How Squirrel Can Warn Us of Danger

Unfortunately, there are some out-of-balance humans who would take advantage of Squirrel's trusting nature and do it harm. And while a Squirrel may be very tolerant of the presence of other Squirrels, it must still be careful not to lose its winter stores to another. One study showed that when it thought it was being watched, a Gray Squirrel dug false holes in which it buried nothing so as to confuse anyone who might try to steal from its cache. This shows that while it is good to have a trusting nature, even Squirrel knows that one should not underestimate the importance of being circumspect in a dangerous world.

Turkey

TURKEY'S MESSAGE:
Trust that your resources will be replenished.

TURKEY'S WARNING:
Treat something of value as the sacred gift that it is.

Behavior and Habitat

Wild Turkeys are opportunistic feeders with broad tastes. They eat nuts, berries, green foliage, grasshoppers, lizards, salamanders, and many other foods. They are powerful flyers, at least for short distances, and most often they roost for the night high in trees. They can also run at speeds of up to 20 miles per hour. Wild Turkeys have excellent vision during the day but don't see as well at night. The domestic Turkey comes from a Mexican variety that was shipped to Europe in the 1500s and returned here a century later.

Wild Turkeys winter together in mixed flocks ranging in size from fewer than a dozen to several hundred birds. In spring, just before the mating season, these flocks divide into three groups: the females, the young males, and the older breeding males. Prior to courtship, the older males are likely to engage in bloody battles with each other. The regional winner then attempts to attract as many females as he can with his grand displays and dances. After mating, the male will leave the female to incubate an average of 12 eggs and to care for her young ones. The Wild Turkey was hunted to near extinction by 1930, but thanks to conservation efforts, there are several million Wild Turkeys roaming the less settled parts of North America.

We live in a rural part of the country, on forested land that is home to Wild Turkeys. The record number we have seen at one time is 27. Just as we opened the door to go outside one day, a mother Turkey strutted out of the tall grass at the edge of the backyard with a line of little ones behind her, followed by three more groupings just like the first. With only inches between them, the four families stretched single-file across the entire length of the yard as they marched along back to the woods. We dared not move, lest they startle into a panicked flurry. What an exciting sighting that was for us avid bird watchers!

How Turkey's Medicine Gifts Help Us

The medicine power of Turkey is renewal. Wild Turkeys were an abundant food source for Native peoples and became one for the early European refugees as well. However, the latter's uncontrolled hunting of them, along with habitat disruption, had at one time virtually eliminated these birds in a number of regions. When reintroduced and managed, their populations recovered rapidly. Is there something you could be doing to secure an abundant future? If Turkey has gobbled its way into your life, it may be there to encourage you to cultivate those renewable resources that benefit your life and your Earthwalk. This care can be as simple as taking the time to give thanks for what you already have.

How Turkey Can Warn Us of Danger

Wild Turkeys were almost eliminated because their existence was taken for granted. As with the passenger pigeon and the buffalo, some people came to believe that certain animals were an endless resource because there seemed to be so many of them. But no resource is limitless, especially if it is not honored and nurtured. Are you relying on something in your life that you expect always to be there, but that you are taking no steps to treat in a sacred way? This can pertain to a human partner, a job, or any other resource that facilitates your life in some way. If you answered "yes" to this question, heed the lesson of Turkey and recognize that everything has limits, and if it is not cared for properly, a thing of value can disappear before you know it.

Turtle

TURTLE'S MESSAGE:
Add gratitude and ceremony to your life.

TURTLE'S WARNING:
Don't get too set in your ways.

Behavior and Habitat

The whole matter of who's who in the world of Turtle can be very confusing. Generally speaking, Turtles are creatures of the water, living in both saltwater and freshwater environments. They have webbed feet or flippers and are excellent swimmers; some have been clocked at over 20 miles per hour. Terrapins are a freshwater species of Turtle who are equally comfortable on land, and the Tortoise is strictly a land dweller, going to water only to drink or bathe. The naming of various species of Turtles and Tortoises is surprisingly unscientific and imprecise, so it is often impossible to tell from their names which is which. The familiar Box Turtle lives on land, some animals named Tortoise swim much of the day, and it is actually the Terrapin that is the usual ingredient in Turtle soup. To further complicate identification, names for members of the Turtle family vary regionally and by continent.

214

Whatever their names, they are reptiles with shells made of separate, bony plates attached to their bodies along the spine, with a few marine exceptions who have tough, leathery skin. All can contract into their hard shells, at least to some degree, to protect themselves against attack. This defense has been effective in Turtle's survival since before dinosaurs roamed the Earth; they have changed very little in over 200 million years of evolution.

Some species of Turtles can weigh as much as 1,000 pounds and live longer than 100 years. Tortoises range in size from 4 to 400 pounds and are also long-lived. Land Tortoises travel slowly, generally no more than half a mile per hour. In cooler climates, Tortoises hibernate for the winter under leaves and in soft soil. Where it's hot, the Desert Tortoise has evolved two sacs within the upper portion of its dome-shaped shell, enabling it to go for many years without drinking water, instead ingesting it entirely from plants. Not even the fearsome Snapping Turtle is aggressive by nature, although it will bite with its powerful jaws if provoked.

How Turtle's Medicine Gifts Help Us

North America is called "Turtle Island" by many Native peoples. Stories tell of a time when there was only water and no place for people and animals to live; some say this was before there was any land at all, and others attribute the absence of land to a flood. According to legend, Turtle made a great sacrifice and invited everyone to come and live on her back. Turtle thus came to be a symbol of the Earth itself.

Rattles made from Turtle shells are believed to invite the spirits of a place into ceremony and to give more energy to sacred songs. If you need to contact the Earth Mother for knowledge or healing, Turtle can be your guide. If Turtle comes ambling onto your path, it could be that you are being asked to accord more respect to the Earth in your daily activities, perhaps even at the cost of some sacrifice. And remember to give to Mother Earth as well as receive from her great bounty.

How Turtle Can Warn Us of Danger

Turtle, for all its legendary wisdom, can get very rigid and set in its ways. If a Tortoise decides a road is part of its territory, it will cross and recross it even if doing so is very dangerous. Sea Turtles will travel for thousands of miles in the oceans to spawn on the same beaches at the same time of year, even though that makes them vulnerable to those who would prey on them. An encounter with Turtle might be a way of advising you to relinquish inflexible ideas about how the world works and how you fit into the grand scheme of things, so that you can experience something new. And by all means, slow down so you can appreciate life and all the wonders of Creation.

217

Vulture

> ## VULTURE'S MESSAGE:
> It's time to clean up a mess.
>
> ## VULTURE'S WARNING:
> Don't have too much chaos in your life.

Behavior and Habitat

Although some species of Vultures will occasionally capture live prey and some even eat plant matter, Vultures feed primarily on carrion. Vultures can digest meat in any stage of decay and are able to withstand diseases that would kill any other creature. They thus perform an essential ecological service by disposing of the remains of decaying animals that could breed diseases harmful to people and wildlife. Their heads are bald so that as they are eating, the bacteria and parasites in their food can't find a new home in their head feathers.

In North America, the Turkey Vulture, with its six-foot wingspan, is the most common. These birds have an extremely keen sense of smell, which they use to locate food. Their sight is also superior, enabling them to spot a meal from thousands of feet above the ground. Vultures can fly effortlessly for hours at a time, without a single flapping of their wings, by gliding

over warm rising pockets of air called thermal updrafts. They do not take time from their clean-up tasks to bother building a nest but are content to tend their eggs on the ledge of a cliff or in the bare hollow of a tree.

The largest Vulture in North America is the California Condor, with its ten-foot wingspan. Unhappily, it now tee-ters on the verge of extinction. It once ranged from British Columbia to Florida, but habitat loss, poaching, and attempts to poison other animal "pests," such as the Coyote, reduced the California Condor population to only 22 birds in 1982. Because it takes two years for a Condor to reach maturity, recovery has been difficult, but dramatic conservation efforts have increased their numbers slightly, to approximately 320, about half of whom live again in the wild.

How Vulture's Medicine Gifts Help Us

Vulture plays a prominent role in many Native American tribal stories. In Cherokee lore, Vulture helped create the mountains with a sweep of its broad wings. In a Hopi story, Vulture was credited with bringing light to the world. Even so, many people today don't like Vultures, thinking their bald heads are ugly, and believing that because they feed on carrion they must be unclean birds. The truth is that Vultures, whose Latin name means "cleanser," are actually themselves quite clean, and the important gift they bring to us is the cleaning up of messes. All too often, humans create physical, emotional, and psychic messes that we then don't want to deal with. Vulture can guide us to the efficient and rewarding elimination of the disorder we have created. If Vulture has come to you, it may be offering to help you resolve a messy situation and transform it into something positive.

How Vulture Can Warn Us of Danger

While cleaning up a mess can be a very positive and healing endeavor, having a lot of sticky situations to remedy all the time may be indicative of another problem. If messes somehow seem to always be around you, eventually you could end up with a reputation for creating or attracting predicaments. Like Vulture, you could find yourself in a position of disfavor—whether deserved or not. If you frequently find yourself weighed down with chaos, heed the warning of Vulture and clean up your act so you can soar on your spiritual wings.

Weasel

WEASEL'S MESSAGE:
Be quick and decisive.

WEASEL'S WARNING:
Don't take more than you need.

Behavior and Habitat

Weasels are small mammals, varying from the five-inch Least Weasel to the fifteen-inch Long-tailed Weasel. Despite their diminutive appearance, Weasels are perhaps the most feared of all small predators. They are voracious eaters and expert nocturnal hunters of small animals, and they are not at all reluctant to attack animals many times their size. Woodchucks, muskrats, gophers, and all manner of rodents and ground-nesting birds are fair game for this mighty little carnivore with its razor sharp teeth. Most species of Weasels are good climbers, and on the ground all move incredibly fast when striking (generally at the jugular vein), though they are not strong long-distance runners.

Weasel's body is shaped like a long, thin tube with short legs, enabling it to maneuver easily inside the small burrows of other creatures, where it is capable of killing every occupant, though it may not be able to eat its entire kill. Weasels can dig burrows for themselves quickly when they need to, but being very opportunistic, they will often move into the den of an animal they have killed and might even line their new den with its fur. Two or three litters a year may each consist of two to ten kittens, which the mother will defend fearlessly.

Northern species of Weasels dress in camouflage, wearing brown fur in the summer and winter white to match the snow (except for the black tips of their tails). Weasels are safe from most predators, but can fall victim occasionally to owls, lynxes, foxes, and larger Weasel relatives, such as the Mink. But even these larger predators must approach Weasel with caution. An eagle was once found with a Weasel skull attached by the teeth to its neck.

How Weasel's Medicine Gifts Help Us

The power that Weasel calls its own is quickness. Many animals are fast over distances, but few can rival the darting speed with which Weasel can move. When Weasel decides the time is right, it can strike with unbelievable agility. If Weasel has zipped into your awareness, it may be saying that you need to move more quickly regarding some aspect of your life. Has an opportunity just presented itself to you? If so, you must act with speed and daring. But whether the correct action is to move toward or away from something depends upon your situation, and is for you to determine.

How Weasel Can Warn Us of Danger

Weasels are wasteful by predatory standards. Quite often they eat only a small portion of their kill and leave the rest. This habit might be less objectionable if the leftovers were out in the open, where scavengers could finish the meal, but usually the remains are left at the bottom of a hole where only the Weasel can go. Weasels have earned a reputation for greed due to their practice of killing much more than they need and frequently eating only the choicest parts. Could Weasel be pointing out that you are being wasteful in some area of your life and are not considering what might benefit others? If so, perhaps you need to learn that such behavior is not in keeping with Nature's patterns of balance.

225

W h a l e

WHALE'S MESSAGE:
Reconnect with your creative, intuitive nature.

WHALE'S WARNING:
Don't let others take advantage of you.

Behavior and Habitat

There are two types of Whales: those with teeth, who are carnivorous, and those with baleen plates, with which they filter in plankton and tiny ocean creatures called krill. Toothed Whales include the Sperm Whale, which can measure up to 65 feet in length, and the strange-looking, tusked Narwhal. The Baleen Whales include Humpbacks, Right Whales, and Blue Whales, which are the largest mammals ever to have lived, measuring over 90 feet and weighing up to 285,000 pounds.

Humpbacks are the most acrobatic and playful of all Whales. They leap out of the water in an action called breaching, roll on one side while waving their fins, and then dive in a variety of techniques. Humpbacks grow up to 50 feet in length and are noted for their extremely long flippers, which can measure up to one third of their body length. They

are present in all oceans, migrating to polar seas every summer to feed on krill and returning to tropical waters in winter to breed. Humpback females give birth once every two or three years to a single calf. Immediately after giving birth, the mother Whale turns around to quickly snap the umbilical cord, then places herself under the newborn calf and lifts it to the surface to take its first breath. A baby Whale must then be taught to swim or it will drown like any other air-breathing mammal!

Whales sing. Their complex songs, believed to be sung to maintain contact with others of their species, change as the Whales migrate, and they vary greatly from species to species. The 180-decibel bellow of the Blue Whale can be heard for over 1,000 miles by another Blue Whale. Throughout the mating season, the voices of Humpback males resonate in long symphonies that can last up to 30 minutes and are then repeated precisely. Amazingly, even though they may be separated by thousands of miles, all male Humpbacks living in the same ocean sing the same song, and that song changes from year to year. Their ability to learn these complex songs, and the fact that Whales rely more on learned behavior than on instinct, are signs of a highly evolved intelligence.

How Whale's Medicine Gifts Help Us

Whales inhabit the oceans, whence life on the Earth arose. They are aquatic mammals whose land ancestors returned to the sacred waters over 100 million years ago. But they still feel the vibrations and hear the songs of Mother Earth, and are thus closely linked to the origins of our life. They hold keys to the past and to ancient knowledge. The power of Whale is to reconnect us with the creative, intuitive, and psychic aspects of our nature. If Whale has breached its way into your vision, it may be saying that you already have within you the knowledge that you need, if you will but listen for the song.

How Whale Can Warn Us of Danger

Whale's size and relative passivity made it an easy and profitable target for human hunters. The Right Whale was so named because it was considered the right Whale to hunt; it was slow and its body floated after death. Whales, much like Buffaloes, fulfilled many human needs, from food to light to heat. Today we no longer need anything from Whales, yet their populations are still in some degree of decline, as hunting continues and pollution of the seas takes its toll. Whale's warning to you may be to not let yourself be exploited or taken advantage of just because you are easygoing or trying to mind your own business. It may be time to move actively out of the way of trouble and to keep a low profile.

Wolf

WOLF'S MESSAGE:
Care for your family and your community.

WOLF'S WARNING:
Don't ignore your own needs.

Behavior and Habitat

Several species of Wolves exist, differing greatly in size from 30 to 150 pounds. Before humans decimated their numbers, Wolves lived in a wide variety of climates from subarctic to subtropical. All of their senses are excellent—well above those of humans. Wolves prey mostly on hoofed animals, such as deer, moose, and elk. They have been known to run distances of 35 miles in a day in pursuit of a meal. They usually hunt in packs, relying largely on endurance to run down weak and older animals; taking the slower ones serves to strengthen the health of the herds they prey on.

Despite their fearsome reputation in movies and literature, Wolves actually prefer to avoid people. As of 2008, there is no documented case of a healthy, wild Wolf ever killing a human in the United States, and in those rare cases where a Wolf did attack a person, human error was generally involved.

With an extremely well-developed societal organization, Wolves act together to hunt and to raise their young. For example, others in an extended family group will bring food home to a nursing mother and will help to care for older pups. There is a rigid hierarchy in Wolf packs, with the alpha male and the alpha female calling the shots. Wolves are seldom aggressive toward each other and rarely engage in actual violence. Only when Wolves are having a dominance struggle, or when a stray tries to infiltrate the pack, will there be blood.

How Wolf's Medicine Gifts Help Us

Wolf's medicine can help you to strike a balance between your own needs and the needs that members of your family or your community want you to fill for them. Wolves are totally loyal to the pack, but they do not surrender their identities to it. Each Wolf will act in a way that is unique to its position in the pack's hierarchy and each will be quite different from all the rest. If Wolf has come into your life in some way, it may be asking you to look at whether you are being too dependent and too giving, or if you are too independent and aloof. With regard to both family and community, there needs to be a balance between the "us" and the "me" parts of your life. You can only do your best for others when you are coming from a well-cared-for and balanced place. Wolf can help you get there.

How Wolf Can Warn Us of Danger

In Wolf terms, it is almost impossible to be too loyal to the pack. In human terms, you can become so devoted to an idea, a group, or a family unit that it harms you, especially if that association is dysfunctional and robbing your power. Loyalty is a fine trait, but if it is negating who you are and what you need, it can be destructive. If Wolf is loping along beside you, it could be there to help you elevate your status in the hierarchy, or to break away and start a pack of your own.

WOLF

Wolverine

DANCING OTTERS AND CLEVER COYOTES

> **WOLVERINE'S MESSAGE:**
> Get tough and fight for yourself.
>
> **WOLVERINE'S WARNING:**
> Don't fight a battle that you can't win.

Behavior and Habitat

Wolverines are the largest members of the Weasel family. They are quite rare and are seldom encountered by humans, especially since they live primarily in the far northern regions of the United States into Canada, and spend most of the day in burrows, emerging at night to hunt. Although they are basically terrestrial animals, Wolverines are very good at climbing trees and are also powerful swimmers.

Wolverines will eat berries, edible roots, and various plants, but flora represent only a small part of their diet. They are tenacious predators who will travel great distances in pursuit of their primary food: any kind of meat. They prey on everything from rodents, rabbits, birds, and fish to animals that are much larger in size, including deer and caribou, especially the weak or injured. This is truly astounding for an animal who averages three feet in length and weighs only 30 to 50 pounds. Wolverines also eat carrion and will even dig into the snow to find hibernating animals.

Despite their squat bodies and short legs, Wolverines can travel quickly, covering 20 or more miles of hilly terrain each night in search of food. One GPS-collared male was tracked as he traveled more than 250 miles in just 19 days. During the month and a half he wore the collar, he crossed eight mountain ranges in Wyoming, Montana and Idaho.

Anecdotes about Wolverine's actions and abilities are extraordinary. They have been credited with superhuman intelligence and, at times, incredible malice. Hunters and trappers have told tales of being stalked by Wolverines who triggered

traps set for other animals, stole the bait, and then fouled the traps with a malodorous spray—not quite as strong as that of skunk, but unpleasant enough. There have been reports of Wolverines breaking into cabins and stealing food, clothes, blankets, and cookware—just about anything they could carry and hide—and destroying whatever they couldn't move. It is said that if a hunter or trapper gets a Wolverine mad at him and lets it get away, his best bet is to leave that part of the country. Often even a full-grown bear or cougar will run

235

rather than compete with this beast for a kill. A mother Wolverine will savagely protect her offspring and will not hesitate to attack even a human.

How Wolverine's Medicine Gifts Help Us

Wolverine is indeed the terror of the North American animal kingdom. Its power is pure aggression; it can make even a badger seem like a rabbit by comparison. Wolverines have a large territory that they patrol looking for food, and they defend that territory from interlopers. If this rare creature has somehow come marauding into your space, its message may be for you to get tough. There are times when we legitimately need to call forth the power and fury of our innate survival instincts. This doesn't have to mean violence in a literal sense, but it may be time for you to draw a line in the proverbial sand and do everything you can to defend that line. Are you in a fight for your life with someone or something? Do you need to protect something or someone very important to you? If so, ask Wolverine to be your guide.

How Wolverine Can Warn Us of Danger

We can sometimes be too aggressive, drawing lines to defend in places where they need not be drawn. Wolverine is consistently characterized as devilish, vicious, gluttonous, and vile. Are you too aggressive when it comes to getting what you need? Are you taking more than your fair share? Do you drive people away when you may really need their help? Wolverine may be warning you to back off from a battle you can't win, or perhaps shouldn't even fight.

ANIMAL ENCOUNTERS

Gary's Encounter with a "Reindeer"

When I decided to leave New York City and move West to live closer to the Earth, my heart was in the right place, but my brain still needed help in the area of acquiring useful information. It seems that being born and raised in New York doesn't prepare one well for a life of outdoor adventure—unless your idea of adventure is taking the subway to work and getting home again without being mugged. I experienced little annoyances while I was driving cross-country, mostly due to ignorance: "Oh, I'll just stop at a motel in central Wyoming when I get tired," "Surely a Dodge Colt can make it through this mud," and the like. But the incident that stands out most on my first cross-country trip happened in Yellowstone National Park.

The start of my visit to Yellowstone should have alerted me that I had some things to learn. In New York, the only wildlife (nonhuman, that is) that one gets to encounter are cockroaches, rats and mice, pigeons and sparrows, and the occasional squirrel. And if it's cold, well . . . you just duck into a coffee shop for some hot chocolate and a bagel. I arrived at Yellowstone in late June, anxious to see the wildlife and just absorb the awesome sights and sounds that the Earth Mother had to offer. I thought I was all prepared to camp out. I had some sandwiches, a nice new tent, a little sleeping pad, and a cotton sheet. It was a beautiful day when I arrived, albeit a little cooler than I had expected, not realizing that Yellowstone is high in the mountains. When night came, it got down to twenty-two degrees and started snowing. I thought, "This can't be happening. It's late June!"

As I tried to start a fire with some wet twigs, two old road maps, and three matches, a park ranger came into camp to inform us that everyone had to move. Some grizzly bears had just wandered into the area and we could be in danger. I laughed and thought it would be great fun to come nose-to-nose with a bear! Since I enjoy cold weather, I survived the night without too much discomfort—and with no bears.

But the next day, as I was enjoying a slow drive through the park and looking at the sights, I saw two deer in a field. Wanting to get a closer look and take a picture of them, I stopped at a pull-off area and started walking across the field. It was then that I noticed a group of about twenty people a good hundred yards from the deer, just watching them. I didn't think much of that and kept heading toward the deer. By the time I got within twenty feet or so, the male was watching me very intently. I was proud that I knew he was the male because he had antlers. (That's one of the things you learn from watching PBS.) What I didn't know from TV, however, was just how large a deer was when you were that close to it. And what huge antlers he had! The deer was about six feet tall and his antlers added another three feet.

I was moving very slowly because I didn't want to scare off the pretty deer and get the people watching mad at me. I was reassuring him—"It's okay, Mr. Reindeer; I won't hurt you"—and waving to him as I edged closer, to within ten feet. I had a wide-angle lens on the camera and I wanted a good picture, so I needed to get close. As I took my picture, he seemed to get startled. His mate was about twenty feet further back and she became quite skittish. The big guy then planted his huge rack of antlers in the ground and flicked dirt my way as he took a couple of quick steps toward me.

I was upset that I had scared the deer and tried not to make any sudden moves. By this time, there were gasps coming from the crowd behind me and I assumed they were angry at me for scaring him. After his two quick steps, he stopped, now about five feet from me, with his head down, looking me in the eyes. I had nothing but admiration and respect for so beautiful a creature and I was trying to communicate that to him and send blessings to both him and his mate. Our eyes were locked for several seconds and then he turned and trotted away, with his mate beside him.

As I made my way back to the car, I was confronted by some of the people who had been watching. One man said, "Y'ur plumb crazy. I thot u wuz a goner fur shur!" I asked him, "From what, a deer?" He shouted, "A deer! Wher'u frum? That wuz a bull Elk guardin' his mate. He wuz about to maul u good. Yep, I thot u wuz a goner fur shur!" He walked away, just shaking his head. I also got several strange stares from other people in the group as I walked to my car. I thought at the time that they were surely overreacting to the danger. But as I asked around and did some research, I determined that under the circumstances and given the aggressive posture the Elk took—especially the motion of his antlers—I should have been banging around in those flicking-dirt antlers like a pin-ball earning extra bonus points.

I attribute my not being attacked to one of several things: One, after looking at me and seeing that I had no fear—and I really felt none since I thought this was Bambi's father—the Elk realized that I was too stupid for him to kill; two, he sensed my admiration and respect for him and his mate as my relations upon the Earth and felt my blessings and silent prayers for their well-being; or three, Great Mystery intervened to save a fool. I think that it was actually a bit of all three that saved me.

What I learned from my close encounter with the Elk is that while one can't go around intentionally doing stupid things or challenging nature, it is possible to be kept safe and protected when you have a pure heart. I also learned that the seemingly inevitable doesn't always have to happen, as the world is a mysterious place and the only real rules are made by Spirit. I now feel a special connection with Elk, and I always try to carry myself with the same kind of pride and power that this animal manifests. I am grateful for his teaching, and the memory of his eyes and the force of his spirit shall stay with me for the rest of my days.

Sherry's Encounter with a Phoebe Family

Gary and I are avid bird watchers. We feed the birds who visit our backyard all year long. We keep binoculars by the back windows so we can observe our feathered friends more closely, along with bird identification books so we can tell who's who. Every February we participate in the Great Backyard Bird Count.

We see lots of different species on a regular basis, including Cardinals, Tufted Titmice, Mourning Doves, Blue

Jays, Nuthatches, Chickadees, Towhees, Grackles, various Sparrows, and a few Starlings. There's a flock of Goldfinches when there's thistle in the feeder, none when it's empty. Seasonally, we also observe Juncos, Robins, Catbirds, Brown Thrashers, Cedar Waxwings, Indigo Buntings, and Hummingbirds. There are occasional visits from Cowbirds and several species of Woodpeckers. Wrens nest in the gourd houses we provide for them. In the woods nearby, we see Crows, Vultures, Turkeys, and Hawks. At night we hear the hooting of Owls.

Our encounter with the Eastern Phoebes occurred early one summer when we returned from a trip to our former home in Kentucky, to discover that a Phoebe had already laid her eggs in a nest she'd built under the front-porch eaves, just above a stone pedestal. Four baby Phoebes soon hatched and, through the window in Gary's office, we watched them grow.

Being rather psychic, Gary had the notion that we should cover the pedestal with something soft, just in case one of the babies fell out of the crowded nest. Shortly after we cushioned the spot with towels, we came home from town one evening to find one of the young ones perched among the towels.

We knew from a good friend, who is a wildlife rehabilitator at the University of Minnesota and an expert on bird behavior, that the popular belief that parent birds will abandon their nest if they detect the scent of humans is incorrect. Birds actually have a poor sense of smell but strong parental instincts. So Gary carefully picked up the little guy, who clutched tightly to Gary's hand, and placed him back in the nest. Perhaps in his excitement with his developing wings, or more likely out of fear, the young bird immediately fluttered to the ground. This sequence was repeated, but this time the Little Peep flapped his wings and skittered across the grass toward a pile of tree branches we had collected after windstorms.

Our friend Paul had also told us that young birds may leave the nest a day or two early, in which case it may be better not to interfere. The parent birds will stay in close attendance, protecting the little one and feeding it on the ground until it can take flight. Not knowing what to do, we just watched intently from Gary's office as the mama bird did indeed feed the little guy on the ground and then coaxed him into the woodpile for the night. Not wanting to risk hurting him by trying to put him back in the nest again, hoping he'd take flight in the next day or so, and figuring he'd be safe for the night among the twigs (since the weather forecast called for clear skies for the next few days), we left him there and went to sleep.

I was awakened at four o'clock the next morning by an unpredicted thunderstorm with heavy rain. My first thought was of the little bird in the woodpile. I didn't know what to do and I didn't want to make matters worse by attempting a rescue in the dark, so I just prayed. I got up and did a smudging ceremony, asking Spirit to protect the little bird among the branches and to stop the rain. A second storm heading our way did pass us by, and before dawn the rain stopped.

At first light, I started watching from the window and saw Mama Phoebe taking juicy bugs to her three babies who remained in the nest. But to my dismay, she completely ignored the woodpile. I was afraid the little one had died and that she somehow knew that.

When I could stand it no longer, I went out to see if I could find him. He was in fact alive, hunkered down at the

243

edge of the woodpile, very wet and shivering from the cold. I took off my jacket and carefully placed the little one—who now looked ever so much smaller than he had the night before—on the shirt, out in the open where Mama would be sure to see him. I had to pry his little talons open because he had latched tightly onto the grass beneath him. When I set him down on my shirt, his mouth opened wide, hoping for a big bug to feed his hungry stomach. I knew then that it would be some time before he could survive on his own. My heart almost broke from my feeling of helplessness.

I went back into the house and watched Mama Phoebe continue to neglect Little Peep. She saw him and even flew to the woodpile, but she wouldn't feed him. I deduced later that she probably knew he would die if he stayed there and she saw no point in expending extra energy when she had three other demanding babies in the nest. It also seemed that in the nest she fed the one that peeped the loudest, and this lone one was quiet, huddled for warmth in the folds of my shirt, still shivering as it started to drizzle again.

In desperation, I decided that his only chance for survival would be if he returned to the nest where he could get dry and warm and where Mama Phoebe could easily feed him. So I pried his little feet away from the shirt he was clinging to and lifted him up to the nest.

By this time, I was beginning to realize that baby birds evidently keep from falling out of the nest by hanging on tightly to the nesting material. So I tried to make sure he had a good foothold before I let go. It worked! This time he was quite content to stay in the nest.

Once inside the house again, I watched Mama Phoebe fly toward the nest half a dozen times and then veer away, evidently confused by the presence again of the lost one. Finally, she landed and began feeding the other three. My heart sank again as she ignored the open mouth of the wet one. Then at last, he must have warmed up enough to get his voice back, and I saw her stuff some food into his gaping beak. Needless to say, my spirit soared! He would survive!

For almost five more days, we watched the Phoebe family. The father bird showed up to help feed the four rapidly growing babies. We delighted in seeing the young ones stretch their wings and squirm around in their increasingly crowded space, and we knew the time would soon arrive for them to fly away.

Then, that afternoon, more drama. I had decided I would write the Phoebe story for a magazine we were publishing and thought it would be fun to include a picture of the four little heads in the nest. So I asked Gary to take a photo. He got in good position, but as soon as he raised the camera, all four young birds flew from the nest, scattering in surrounding tree branches. "Oh, dear," I thought, "what have I done?" I feared that the parents weren't ready for the babies to fly, or they wouldn't have still been in the nest. Night was approaching. What would become of them?

Through the window, we watched the parents locate all the young ones in the trees and bring them food. After a short while, we discovered all four of the fledglings perched together in one tree, and laughed to see each facing a different way, as if to honor the four directions—or more likely to keep watch. Three were within inches of each other on the same branch, while the fourth was by itself on a branch just above the others. Before dark, we saw the whole family in a tree in the field just beyond the fence. Again, three of the young ones were perched on the same branch, with the fourth slightly aloof. We had to wonder if this was our Little Peep, dancing to a different drumbeat because of his unique experiences.

They all must have spent the night in that tree, since early the next morning they were still there, now practicing flying. We watched them flit between the tree and the fence and then down to the ground and back up again, no doubt to strengthen their wings. We realized that the young Phoebes, being flycatchers, would have to learn fancy flight maneuvers before they could adequately feed themselves.

They mastered flight in short order, and in the days that followed, we occasionally saw young Phoebes flying about in the yard. As far as we know, all six birds survived and lived good lives, creating more Phoebes to follow in their flight paths. We're very happy believing that was the case.

I learned several valuable lessons from this intensely emotional encounter with the Phoebes. From Little Peep, I learned that it is advisable to be sure you are ready for a major life experience before venturing beyond the safety of the nest. From Mama Phoebe, I learned that it is important to overcome confusion caused by the unexpected and to keep on one's path, doing the work that needs to be done. From Spirit, I learned to have faith. Perhaps it took a drenching to subdue the little one's rambunctiousness so he would be willing to stay where he needed to be until the right time came to move on. And from the happy ending I learned that sometimes it is okay to help Mother Nature out when circumstances warrant. But from my fear about the premature departure of the young ones from the nest, I also learned that interfering with Nature for selfish reasons instead of for the good of the animals can be a dangerous thing.

I must confess that, contrary to Paul's warning that it is not good to bond with wild animals, I did come to feel very close to these little critters, especially the almost-lost one. Gary and I joked about being their "godparents," so we were both very glad they all survived. Thank you, Great Spirit!

TWO ORIGINAL STORIES IN THE NATIVE AMERICAN STYLE

Written by Gary Buffalo Horn Man

The Story of Sharp Point and the Rabbit

Long ago, when the Earth was young, the nations of animals and two-leggeds lived in harmony. All beings had a special place in the Sacred Hoop of Life. Some animals, like Wolf, were given gifts that made them hunters. Through a sacred agreement that the animal nations and the two-leggeds all had with each other, the hunters helped keep other animal nations strong by taking only the weak and the old. Some of the nations of animals who didn't hunt were given defenses to protect them; Turtle had its shell and Skunk, its strong scent. Still others, like Rabbit, were given the gift of multiplying quickly to keep their nations strong. Other animals hid well, some ran fast, some flew. Every being lived according to the gifts given to it by Creator.

Each animal was given a different place to live. Beaver inhabited the ponds it made. Deer liked the forested areas. Eagle lived high in the mountains, along with Bighorn Sheep. Gopher lived in the ground, Alligator in the marshes, Otter in the rivers and the seas. Whale swam in the deep oceans; Snake dwelt in the hot places, and Snowshoe Hare in the cold. Antelope roamed the plains, and Cougar, the hills.

The two-leggeds who lived during this time were in balance and harmony with each other, the Earth Mother, and all upon her. While there were contests of skill and bravery among different nations, there were no wars. There were many different two-leggeds in many different parts of the world, for they could live on almost all the land. The gift given to them by Creator that made this so was their intellect. It enabled them to speak, remember, and teach each other better than other animals could. They were able to create tools better than other animals, and from these tools they made many things to help them stay alive. Intelligence was truly a great gift given to the two-leggeds by Creator, but a dangerous one also. Eagle, who could see far and wide, knew that the shouting of the mind could sometimes drown out the whispers of the heart.

At this time there lived a young man whose name was Sharp Point, for he was a good flint knapper with excellent skills in hunting contests. Alone on his journey of manhood and far from his people, he set up camp early one day in a small clearing. He was very hungry because he had walked far that day. Part of the challenge of Sharp Point's journey was that he must provide food for himself, so he prayed in a sacred way for an animal willing to give up its life so he could go on.

Rabbit heard the young man stirring in his camp and grew curious, since two-leggeds had not been to this part of the country for many moons and Rabbit had never seen one before. Rabbit hopped quietly through the bushes and stuck his nose through some brambles to get a look at this creature. Sharp Point, being a very good hunter, saw Rabbit.

He said to Rabbit, "Aho, Brother. Thank you for coming in answer to my prayer, for I am hungry. You do not seem old or lame, though, but I am hungry, so I will eat you."

He took his lance and threw it at Rabbit. Now, Rabbit hadn't meant to be anyone's dinner. He was just curious about this two-legged, so when Rabbit saw the lance pointed in his direction, he turned around and ran through the bushes and up a hill. Even though Sharp Point was a good hunter, Rabbit ran so fast that the lance only grazed his back leg. Rabbit screamed at the two-legged and looked around for some shelter where he could hide. Rabbit saw a small cave and figured that he could hide there, where it was dark, until the two-legged went away. What Rabbit didn't consider was that the blood dripping from his wound would leave an easy trail to follow.

Sharp Point felt sorry that he had only hurt Rabbit, as this was not how animals were to be hunted according to the sacred ways he had been taught. So, very concerned, he followed the blood trail to the cave, intent on ending Rabbit's pain as quickly as possible. He found Rabbit hiding in the back of the cave. Rabbit asked Sharp Point, "Why are you trying to kill me?"

Sharp Point answered, "Why, to eat you, of course. You came in answer to my prayer for food."

Rabbit shouted, "No, I didn't! I just wanted to see what a two-legged looked like. I don't want to be your dinner!"

This confused Sharp Point greatly. He said to Rabbit, "I only injured you when I should have killed you quickly, so I understand that you are upset. But I am trying now to honor the Sacred Balance of all things."

Rabbit said, "You are right to honor the Sacred Agreement among all creatures, but I am not old or weak. I wasn't meant to be your dinner. Let me go. I will heal from this scratch."

Sharp Point thought about this. He believed that perhaps Rabbit should be let go, but he was very hungry. He thought to himself that it was only his bad aim that had allowed Rabbit to live. Besides, Rabbit must have come in answer to his prayer. And his wound was probably worse than Rabbit thought; he would probably die anyway. So Sharp Point killed Rabbit and took him back to his camp to eat him. When he arrived there, Squirrel was sitting in the middle of his camp.

Squirrel declared, "How rude of you to offer prayers for food and then leave! I came in answer to your prayer. I am old and tired and have had a good life. You may eat me."

It was then that Squirrel saw Rabbit dead in Sharp Point's hand.

"What have you done?" exclaimed Squirrel. "I knew Rabbit. He was young and strong, not meant for you to kill."

Sharp Point replied, "I thought he had come in answer to my prayer and I was very hungry. I thought he was to be my meal."

"You have done a bad thing, my friend. We must ask mighty Eagle what to do now, for Eagle flies high near Creator and sees and knows much."

They did a ceremony to call Eagle and Eagle came. After hearing the tale, Eagle was silent for a long time. Then she asked, "What was in your mind and your heart, Sharp Point, at the exact moment when you killed Rabbit? That is what matters most."

Sharp Point thought for a long while. Each time he thought he had the answer, he looked up and met Eagle's gaze. And that gaze pierced deep into him and he knew that his answer was wrong. Finally he came to an answer that he didn't like very much, but when he looked up at Eagle, he knew this answer to be true.

"I didn't believe Rabbit when he said that he was not to be my meal. I thought that I knew better than he. I was hungry and I did not listen inside myself." Sharp Point hung his head sadly as he spoke.

Eagle said, "Yes, that is what was in your heart." Eagle paused and looked up at the sky. "Creator made me to see long and far, and I see that this marks the start of what must be. A time will come when two-leggeds will think that they, above all others, know best. They will ignore the voices of the beings around them. There will be a great battle. It will not be between people or animals or trees or stones, though they will all suffer greatly. The battle will be between the two-leggeds' heads and the two-leggeds' hearts. This war will decide the paths of all who live upon the Earth Mother. Go now. Remember the sacred ways, though I foresee that many other two-leggeds will forget."

"Is there anything that I can do to make up for my callous action? Is there some way to prevent this?" Sharp Point pleaded. Eagle said, "Many gifts will come to your peoples so that they can remember the sacred ways and not act out of selfishness—gifts of ceremony, a sweat lodge to purify the body and spirit, a pipe with which to talk with Creator, medicine songs and dances, and much more—but nothing can prevent this battle. It will be long after your lifetime when it is decided, but share these words with the people and tell them that no matter what happens, they must remember the sacred ways and honor the ceremonies. Remember. . . ." Eagle took off, a golden streak against the bright blue sky, with Rabbit in her talons.

Sharp Point did share these words with the people. He traveled his whole life and shared with two-leggeds the world over this knowledge that he had been given. Some heard and remembered to keep the sacred ways. Many others forgot his words and Eagle's prophecy. The battle continues to this day.

Respect Your Relations

This story takes place a long time ago, when the world was as fresh as a spring rain. Being the newest of Creator's beings, the two-leggeds needed a great deal of help from our older and wiser Brothers and Sisters of the animal nations. So Creator gave humans the ability to understand the languages spoken by all of our relatives. Thus when we were hungry, we could ask Bear to show us some good berries to eat. When we were sick, we could ask Badger to show us roots with strong medicines. And when we were sad, Coyote could lift our spirits with a story.

One day, when the people were very busy getting ready to plant their crops of corn, beans, and squash, Squirrel came to the village to ask for some help. The branch where she had built her fine lodge had broken and her home was now in shambles on the ground. Since the people were so good with their hands, they could make the rebuilding task go quickly. Her babies would soon need a place to be born. But the people said they were far too busy and told Squirrel that they would have to help her later. Squirrel was shocked, for she had always gladly helped the people find acorns and nuts to eat. She turned away and off she ran, shaking her bushy tail. She began rebuilding her nest alone; the people forgot to come.

Some time passed, and Crow called on the people for help in cleaning pine sap out of some bright feathers he couldn't reach, before it hardened into black goo. Again the people said that they were too busy, but if Crow would wait until they were done with their tasks, they would help him later. Crow stared in disbelief, then shook his head from side to side as he flew off, for he had always hurried to the people after his travels to bring them news of migrating herds they could hunt for food.

Shortly after that, a third animal relative came to the people for help. It was Frog. He had gotten his long tail twisted around a stick and he needed the people's help to untie it, so he would be able to burrow into the mud for the winter. Again the people looked to their own needs first and said to Frog, "Later, Brother. This is the time of our harvest and we cannot stop to help you now." It made Frog sad that the people showed so little appreciation for the many songs he had taught them to sing to the Spirits. Silently he hopped off, dragging the stick behind him.

Later in the season, when the animals got together in their great Council, as they did every year before the snows came, Squirrel told her story of how the two-leggeds failed to help her rebuild her lodge. Crow then told of how they wouldn't take time to help him clean his pretty feathers. Then Frog spoke of the troubles with his tail and how the two-leggeds would not interrupt their work to come to his aid. All of the animals were very upset by the humans' disregard for their needs, and they thought about this matter long and hard.

Eagle, who was well-respected for her clear sight, spoke first. "My friends, we have all sacrificed for the two-leggeds and have tried to help them because they are young and have not yet discovered all the strong Medicines that we have. But they now take for granted the help we give them. I propose that, if all of you agree, we ask Creator to take away their gift of being able to hear and understand our counsel. That way, when they want to ask us for help, they will have to come to us with respect, and they will be required to listen very well and to hear in new ways."

The animals agreed to Eagle's plan, and so it came to be that humans can understand the animals only when we go to them with respect in our hearts and listen well for their teachings. To this day, Squirrel, with her messy lodge, chatters to remind us. And Crow, with his jet-black feathers, caws to remind us. And Frog, with his tail now gone, sings to remind us: Be respectful of all our relations. Aho!

THE SMUDGING CEREMONY

Following an encounter with an animal relative, or before you call on one for guidance, you might find that a smudging ceremony will help with the process of determining what it has to teach you. This Native American way of praying can open your mind to the reason that an animal has appeared to you in some form, and can help you to interpret in a meaningful way the message or warning the animal is trying to impart.

Smudging is a cleansing ceremony that has been used in many traditions throughout history. Widely diverse cultures from all over the Earth have discovered power in working with the smoke from burning herbs and incense. Smell is the sense that connects us to a deep, instinctive part of the brain. Certain scents have the power to change our energies and trigger emotions.

Beyond that, the Native American smudging ceremony adds a dimension of prayerful thanksgiving and respect for the many varied aspects of Creation. The purpose of smudging is to cleanse yourself, your objects, and/or a place. Many people smudge to start the day, as a preamble to another ceremony, or before and after a serious discussion. After a smudging ceremony, it is likely that you will feel energized and the rest of your day will go well.

According to what we have been taught, certain plants have entered into a sacred agreement with us two-leggeds. In exchange for our respectful treatment of them as representing the element of Earth, they will give up their lives so we can use their smoke to stay cleansed and in balance. This means we are to harvest the herbs with honor, asking permission and giving thanks, taking only what we need and not permanently damaging any plants. Smudging before harvesting the sacred herbs is recommended.

We have been taught to perform the smudging ceremony in the manner described here. You are free to follow this ritual, learn another ceremony, or create one that feels right to you. We believe that no one way is right or wrong. With ceremony, it is above all one's sacred intent that opens the door for the powers to work with us.

Herbs commonly used for smudging are sage (desert or white sage, not culinary), which dispels negativity; sweetgrass, which evokes positive energy; cedar or juniper, both of which provide balance; and lavender, which has a calming effect. Any of these herbs may be combined, but we suggest that you first try them one at a time to better connect with the unique powers of each one.

You will also need an abalone shell or similar shell or bowl, thick enough to resist heat; matches, which are less likely than a lighter to burn your fingers; and a feather or fan of feathers. Ideally, the feather(s) will have come to you directly or have personal meaning for you. Feathers acknowledge the winged ones who dwell in the sky, and they call in the element of Air.

Put the abalone shell in front of you and thank it, silently or aloud, for being there to help you honor the gifts of

Grandmother Ocean and to invite the element of Water into the ceremony. Place the herb(s) you will be using in the shell, thanking each as you hold it. They have died so you could have this sacred smoke. This should not inspire guilt, but rather gratitude for their sacrifice.

Next, light the smudge mix. As you bring forth the flame, thank Father Sun, the source of the element of Fire, for coming to help you with this ceremony. Make sure that some of each plant you have put into the bowl gets lit, so that the smoke will contain all the energies you have chosen to work with. Fan the fire gently with your feather until the herbs are burning enough to create sufficient smoke. Then use the feather to put out the flame with one or two quick passes. If the smudge looks like it is going out, fan it vigorously until it is smoking well again. If it does go out, it is fine to relight it.

Now, cupping your hands, catch some smoke and bring it in toward your heart. Catch more smoke and pass it over your head and down your neck. Then with each hand, one at a time, pass the smoke down the opposite arm and hand. Then, using both hands, bring more smoke toward your solar plexus and down your legs to the ground. This process cleanses our hearts, minds, and bodies and helps us to be centered and grounded. While you are doing this, it is good to envision the smoke carrying away any cares or physical injuries.

You can now smudge any objects you wish to by passing them through the smoke from all four directions, starting with the East and going clockwise. Ask that the object be purified for your use or giveaway. You can also smudge a house or room that might need to be cleared of stagnant energy. Move around the space, including corners, with the burning smudge, and use your feather to push any negative energies out through an open door or window.

If you are smudging with other people, smudge yourself first and then hold the shell by its edges for the others to smudge. We recommend that you not use your feather to smudge another person so that there will be no confusion with a feather blessing ceremony, used for healing, that relies on the movement of energy in a certain way.

When you are done, let the ashes cool completely and give them back to the Earth with care; they are now going to become soil from which new life arises. Show respect for this part of the ceremony also by emptying the ashes thoughtfully, again thanking the Four Elementals for their assistance with your prayers. And as you pray, giving thanks and asking for what you need, be sure to listen, too. Listen to what is inside of you and what is all around you. What the voices say may provide keys to greater understanding. Communication does not happen if one only talks and never listens.